Memories of a Gamekeeper's Son

Suffolk farmworkers harvesting barley before the introduction of the reaper-binder, a photograph by Peter Henry Emerson. Great pride was taken in the way the work was done, the best men setting a high standard for the less skilled to attain if they could.

Memories of a Gamekeeper's Son

Edward Turner

MALTHOUSE PRESS
1997

First published by Malthouse Press, 1997.

ISBN 0 9522355 6 0

British Library Cataloguing-in-Publication Data

A catalogue record for this book is
available from the British Library.

Printed in Great Britain by
The Ipswich Book Company Ltd.,
The Drift, Nacton Road, Ipswich.

Contents

Publisher's note

EDWARD Turner is, as will become apparent to the reader, the son of Tom Turner, for more than forty years Head Gamekeeper to Lord Iveagh on the Elveden estate. Tom was in his eighties when Lord Iveagh persuaded him to set down his memories of life on a great sporting estate and arranged for their publication in 1954 as *Memoirs of a Gamekeeper*; in a short foreword Lord Iveagh touchingly referred to Tom as 'my old friend'.

Edward retired in 1967 after twenty-one years in the Estate Office and an even longer period working in the estate game larder under his father. He had left school at thirteen to work on the farm, and can recall details of a way of life that is now entirely gone.

In his retirement he sought to emulate his father by writing down his reminiscences, filling notebook after notebook with stories of life in a village community and work on a great estate that now seem to belong to an almost incomprehensible past. Thanks to his son Neville and his daughter-in-law Gillian his notes were transferred to a word processor and prepared for publication.

Father and son together have produced a record covering a century and stretching through five reigns. In Tom Turner's case the reference to the Monarch is no irrelevance, for two reigning Kings and a future King shot at Elveden in his time, and he was proud that when King George VI came to Elveden during the Second World War on more serious wartime business he took the time to talk to him about the situation on the estate.

The two books are very different. Tom's is a book about sport, and about the part the gamekeeper plays in preparing for the enjoyment of others; Ted's is a much more personal chronicle of life on the Elveden estate. The two are complementary, and together they make up a record of great historical and social importance.

Author's Note

I would like to thank my son Neville and my daughter-in-law, Gill, for the many hours spent at the word processor and for all their help and encouragement over the years. I finally got past the earthquake, Gill!

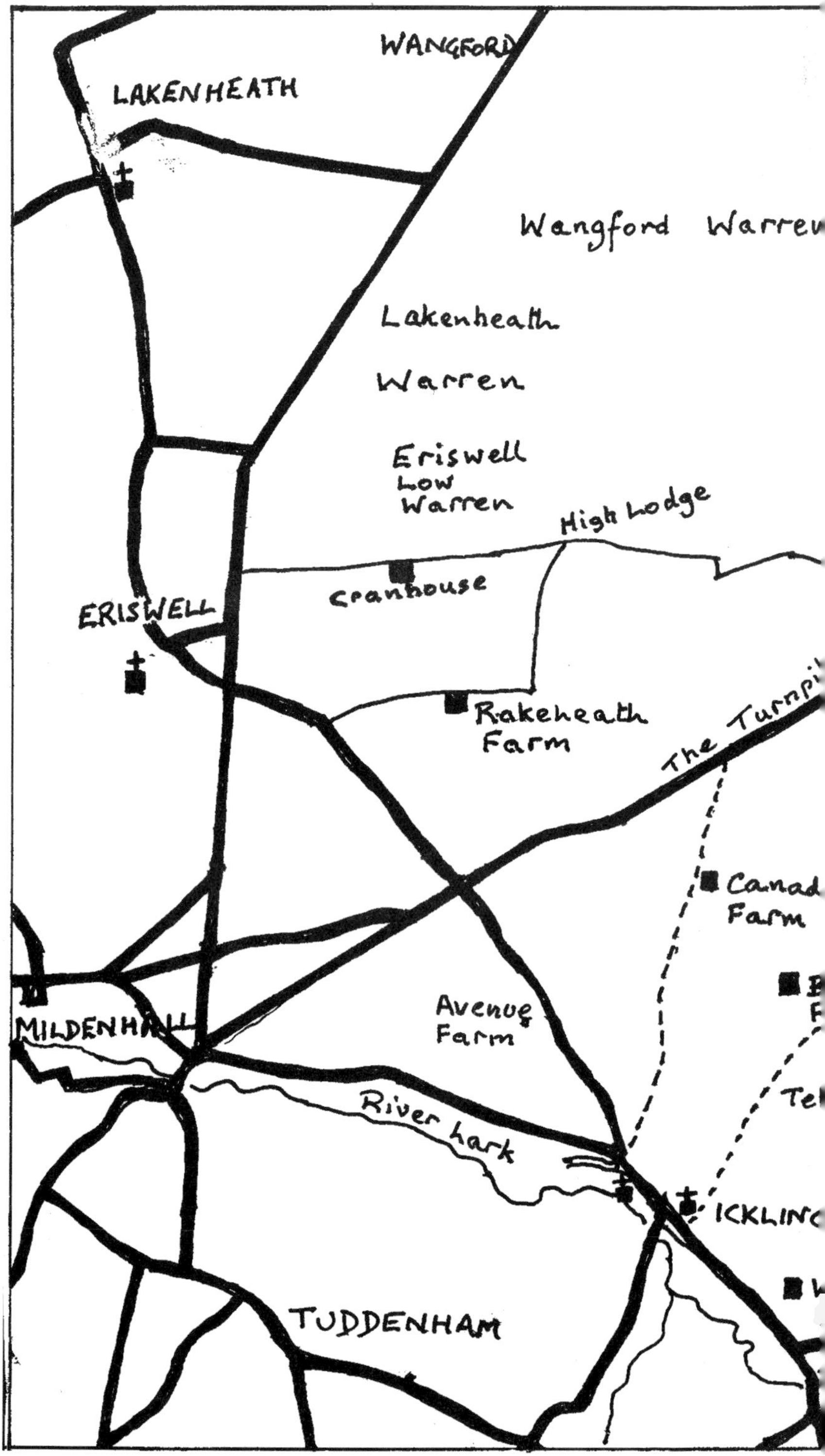

WANGFORD

LAKENHEATH

Wangford Warre

Lakenheath Warren

Eriswell Low Warren

High Lodge

Cranhouse

ERISWELL

Rakeheath Farm

The Turnpi

Canad Farm

Avenue Farm

MILDENHALL

Te

River Lark

ICKLINC

TUDDENHAM

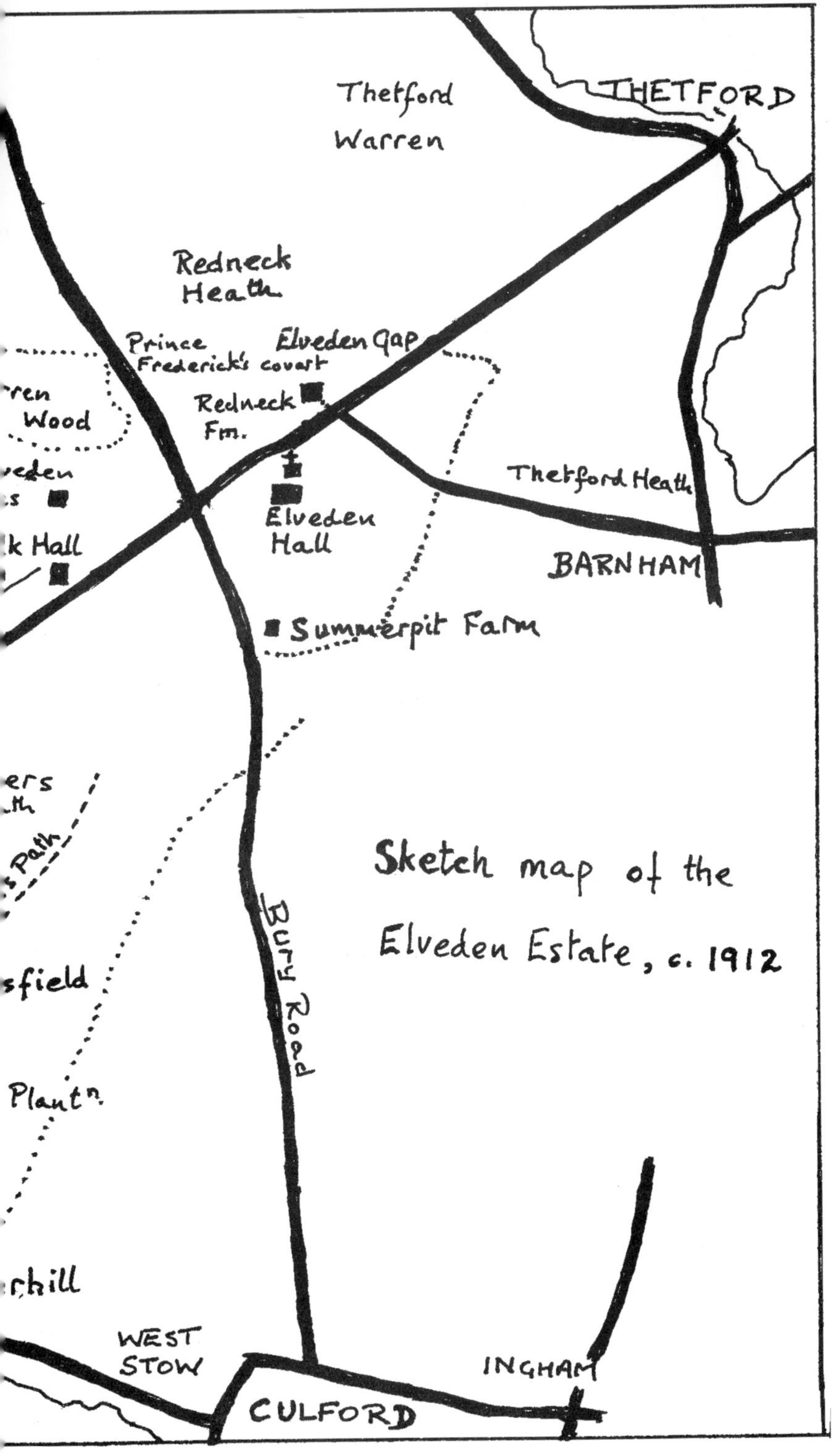

Thetford Warren

THETFORD

Redneck Heath

Prince Frederick's covert

Elveden Gap

ren Wood

Redneck Fm.

eden s

k Hall

Elveden Hall

Thetford Heath

BARNHAM

Summerpit Farm

ers th

s Path

Bury Road

sfield

Plantn.

chill

WEST STOW

CULFORD

INGHAM

Sketch map of the Elveden Estate, c. 1912

Cranhouse 1

MY FAMILY has been involved in the life of the Elveden Estate for several generations. My father, Thomas William Turner, was a gamekeeper on the estate all his life, and my grandfather, Samuel Turner, was a shepherd.

My father was born in May, 1868, at Spark's Farm, Eriswell, close to the edge of the Fens a little over two miles south of Lakenheath. He has told of hearing his parents talking of the hard times that their parents had passed through[1],of how when things were particularly bad they had to eat rye bread, which would be very dark and sticky inside the loaf.

He recalled that in his boyhood the chief fuel was turf, cut from the local fens in the spring. Large families were then the rule, and they had to be maintained on a wage of ten shillings a week.

When he was seven my father saw the owner of the Elveden Estate, H.H. the Maharajah Duleep Singh, partridge shooting in a field at Eriswell. Those were the days of muzzle loaders; the Maharajah had three double-barrelled guns and two loaders who, with their blue and green coats and waistcoats, powder flasks and leather shotbags, made a great impression on him. 'When I grow up to be a man,' he thought, 'I'll be a gamekeeper if I can.'

He was taken on as assistant to one of the keepers when he was sixteen, and at twenty-one was promoted to under keeper. He was later put in charge of Napthen's Beat.

The Maharajah died in 1893, and the following year the estate was bought by Lord Iveagh. The change of ownership had relatively little impact on those who lived on the estate, which continued to be managed as a sporting estate. My father said once that he reckoned he

[1] *Memoirs of a Gamekeeper (Elveden, 1868-1953)*, by T.W. Turner. Geoffrey Bles, 1954.

had seen all the best-known shots in the country at Elveden at one time or another.

When my father married Emma Susan Reeder in 1897 he moved from Napthen's Beat to Sugarloaf Beat, quite close to where he had been born at Eriswell. They moved into Cranhouse, a double dwelling on Sugarloaf Beat. Their neighbours were Mr. and Mrs. Walter Ranns, a horsekeeper and his wife. When the Ranns moved to Canada Farm Mr. and Mrs. Edgar Wright moved in next door; later on they, too, moved to Canada Farm when Mr. Wright became foreman there.

My brother Arthur William was born in May, 1898, followed by Thomas Russell in June, 1899, and Ian Hamilton in August, 1900. I was born on Trafalgar Day, 21st October, 1902, and was duly baptized in Eriswell Church. My sister Frances May was born in March, 1905, and then another sister, Olive Dorothy, in April, 1907.

My earliest recollection is of attending a church service with my grandmother Turner, who lived at The Square, in Eriswell. Wearing her long black dress, which swept the ground as she walked, she took me by the hand and led me to church. When seated in the pew I was sternly told to be quiet and sit quite still. Grandma's word was law in those days.

At about this time, the headmistress of Eriswell School arranged with my mother to see me before we met for the first time at school; she felt it made it easier for a child to know her before starting school.

Mother set out, with me in the pram, to meet Miss Tong half way; it was about two miles from Cranhouse to Eriswell. We duly met, Miss Tong smiled and spoke to me, but I said nothing. She then offered me a penny, but I would not take it and instead let it fall into the bottom of the pram. 'Never mind, I shall know him when he comes to school,' Miss Tong said.

Mother and I watched Miss Tong walk away, then mother said to me, 'You were a naughty little boy to let me down like that, you didn't even say thank you!' The reason was that I was so very shy.

The time came when I was old enough to accompany my brothers in the various activities boys get up to. When they told me they had found a robin's nest I couldn't wait to see it. The nest was in a scots fir hedge. My brothers lifted me up so that I could see, and I grasped some twigs so that I could pull myself a little higher in order to see inside the nest. The twigs snapped, and my other hand, already in the nest to feel the eggs, tilted the nest far enough to allow the eggs to fall to the ground and crack. I was very worried, because I had often been told by father not to touch any birds' nests. The robin's was the most sacred, and the penalty for interfering with one was a broken arm. I was to remember this later.

October came and it was time for me to start school. My eldest brother Arthur took my hand in his and placed both our hands in the pocket of his winter coat, to keep my hand warm and to help me along. Our route led us along a private road as far as the Brandon Road, which we crossed, then we took a short cut across a field which led us to the school on the Lakenheath Road. Arthur delivered me to Miss Tong, then another teacher took charge of me and some other youngsters. I was soon beginning to form the letters of the alphabet and learning how to shape figures.

When the warmer weather arrived we were allowed to eat our packed lunches outside. The boys chose to sit on a flat bricked area of the playground which bordered a ditch, allowing us to dangle our legs over the edge. Below our legs two pipes appeared, every now and then emitting a stream of water. What we did not know was that the pipes led from the school lavatories! One day a farm foreman working on a field near the ditch suggested that we find a more hygienic place to eat our food!

Nearby was a pit that had been filled with cut green clover, which had a vile smell. This, we were told, was a silage pit.

About a year later Dad bought an iron mangle with two large wooden rollers to help dry the linen on wash days. One evening Arthur volunteered to turn the handle, so I offered to feed in the sheets. As usual, anywhere Arthur would go I wanted to go, and after a little practice I was getting on quite nicely. Quite suddenly, I got the sheet a little askew and realized the middle finger of my left hand was beginning to be wound into the rollers, I shrieked in pain. Arthur immediately reversed the handle and released me, but my finger had been split open.

My dad biked to Eriswell to borrow Harry Mizen's pony and cart to take me to Dr. Glazier's surgery in Mildenhall. The doctor dressed and

Pheasant rearing pens on Sugarloaf Beat about 1900, with the author's father in the middle and "Daddy" Baker on the left.

bandaged the split finger, and I was brought home and put to bed; my finger became the centre of attention for a few days.

Another job we boys had to do was to go to the rearing hut situated amongst a belt of tall trees on Dad's beat at Sugarloaf. Our task was to break the shells off scores of hard-boiled hens' eggs which were cooked in big boilers outside the hut on a fire of sticks, to be used mixed with meal to feed pheasants on the rearing fields. We soon got the knack of hitting the eggs on the hut floor and rolling them so the shells came off easily. To begin with we ate some of the eggs, but we soon found that a few mouthfuls were enough!

One day my brother Ian came rushing into the house while we were having tea and said, 'Come quick Dad, there's something outside in the nettles, I think it's either a lion or a hedgehog!' Dad and I went out, returning in fits of laughter a few moments later to tell the others that the 'lion' had turned out to be an old white hen scratching for food. Ian had got his idea about lions from Dad, who, when he took his gun out with him, would say, 'I better take my gun, I might see a lion!'

Sometimes when returning from school, if we were lucky, we would see 'Daddy' Baker by the lodge on the Brandon Road. He was a cheerful elderly Game Department employee who went daily with a watercart to take water to the pheasant rearing hut in Sugarloaf Wood. With sacks thrown over the filler hole of the tank to prevent splashing, we would clamber up and ride on top; a third class ride was better than a first class walk!

We all jumped off at the rearing hut, where Dad and other young men were preparing the night feed for the birds. On this particular day, no doubt to amuse us, someone suggested we placed a bag across the rideway to see who could jump it. Jim Wright from High Lodge jumped first and failed, as he hit the bag with his feet. I was keen to try so ran up and jumped. Not only did I hit the bag but fell back on my right arm and heard a loud crack. Hearing my cry of anguish, Dad rushed forward, picked me up, and placed me over his left shoulder so my damaged arm was hanging free. He carried me home and mother put me to bed.

Dad had a quick tea, then cycled to see Dr. Pickworth in Lakenheath, told him what had happened and asked him to visit me.

The doctor came in his car the next morning, examined my arm and said, 'It's only a greenstick fracture.' He told Dad to obtain a piece of cord and tie a half-brick to it for me to carry around during the day to keep my arm straight! This I did for six weeks, seeing the doctor only once during this time. I also had to stay away from school during this period. The robin had been avenged!

The author with his sisters Olive Dorothy (Doll) and Frances May (Maggie) in front of their house at Icklingham about 1912.

On the move! 2

THERE came the time when my father was put in charge of Icklingham Village Beat, at the southern extremity of the estate. He was also given overall charge of three other beats which were looked after by two brothers, Avenue Beat, where the keeper was James Dorling, and Canada and Bernersfield Beats, of which the keeper was Bill Dorling.

On the morning we moved from Cranhouse Dad and my brother Arthur went ahead of the rest of the family and walked with the wagon and horses conveying our furniture and household belongings to our new home at Icklingham.

It was a bitterly cold morning and snow was falling heavily. The head keeper's groom, Mr. William Alderton, from Elveden, had fitted frost studs to his horse's shoes to prevent them from slipping on the icy surface. He arrived at Cranhouse in good time and picked up my mother, brother Russell and myself in the high yellow cart. Russ and I sat on the floor in the back, wrapped in horse rugs, and my mother and my sisters, May and Dorothy, sat beside Mr. Alderton, sharing his knee rug. Our other brother, Ian, was staying with our grandmother in Eriswell.

As we progressed along the private drive to Gibson's Lodge and down past Canada Farm the weather worsened, and when we began to descend the steep hill towards Icklingham my mother became nervous and asked Mr. Alderton to walk the horse, which he did.

At last we reached our destination and pulled in through the wide yard doors and unloaded. We found someone had thoughtfully lit the fire, for which we were very grateful. About half an hour later, a knock came at the door; it was Mrs. James Dorling, wife of the keeper on the Avenue Beat, who had walked through the snow from Avenue Cottages, where she lived with her husband. Apologising for being late, she said that if she had not worn a pair of her husband's thick woollen stockings over her own shoes to prevent her slipping, she would not have managed to get to us at all. Before long my father and Arthur arrived with the other wagon containing the furniture, which many hands helped to set out into some semblance of order.

We children were warned about the possibility of falling down the three steps into the back kitchen, where there was a large sink, which we had never had at Cranhouse. The well with its roller, handle and metal buckets, was situated just outside the back door. First thing each morning my father would draw two pails of water, placing one beside the sink and one inside the door as a reserve, with a small metal scoop with a wooden handle next to it. Waste water drained into a disused well outside. A tall double chimney above the kitchen served both the kitchen range and a dutch oven.

If one lost a pail down the well the blacksmith, Mr. Robert Harding, would lend an iron hook device attached to a length of cord sufficient to reach the bottom of the well. The time came when Dad lost a pail, so the grapple was borrowed and we children watched him dangling it down the well, trying to catch the handle of the pail. He made a number of attempts to retrieve the pail before he was successful.

Our large kitchen table, underneath which we boys used to play at Cranhouse, was put into the middle room where our fireplace was; this location was the hub of our daily activities. In this living room there was a large dresser opposite the fireplace, with two large drawers below the shelves and cupboards beneath. Large oak beams, black with age, spanned the living-room ceiling and rested on oaken posts set into the outer walls. The spaces between were filled with wattle and daub; that is, sticks nailed across the studwork with clay daubed on it.

In this same room, on the side where the sun never shone, was a small pantry, three steps just inside the door leading down into it; on the outside wall there was a small window covered with perforated zinc to keep out the flies. Outside a shallow hole had been dug, because the pantry window was below ground level.

I always had a weakness for condensed milk. I watched my mother place the opened tin, quite high, on a pantry shelf, and discovered if I stood on the top step leading down to the pantry I could just reach the tin and stick my finger in, scoop out some milk and lick it off. Of course, I gave myself away by keeping on until the tin was nearly empty, when my mother discovered what I had been up to and scolded me soundly.

On breadmaking days the bread dough would be placed in a large earthenware bowl in front of the fire to prove, and I was instructed to watch to see if the dough was rising. From time to time I would gently lift the corner of the cloth covering the bowl to watch the progress of the dough. I spent a long time absorbed in this 'important' task. I didn't realize until later that it was Mother's way of keeping me out of mischief.

Between the kitchen sink and the dutch oven stood a large copper, which had to be filled with water early every Monday morning and lit so that the water boiled ready for washing the linen. My dad would contrive to have some old, dead, dry broom faggots, thick enough to last some time and give a fierce heat. The same fuel was ideal for both the ovens.

The large end room was more modern, being an addition to the original old house. Here my father's armchair was placed on one side of the fireplace and my mother's smaller chair on the other.

This room was only used for special occasions.

With a very thick thatch, the building was remarkably warm during the winter and cool during the summer.

The 'privvy', a little hut with its large oval pail beneath the wooden framework, was near the garden wall, next to the stables. Newspapers torn into small sheets were hung on a nail near the 'seat'.

We had arrived at Icklingham on 2nd March, my sister May's birthday, which meant that Dad soon had to begin to clear some ground in order to plan his garden. Starting to prepare a vegetable garden outside the kitchen window, he re-routed a pipe so it would

The author's mother, Emma Susan Turner, née Reeder.

carry the sink drainage to a disused well at the opposite corner of the garden, covering the well with stout boards for safety.

As the weeks went by Dad, knowing how fond my mother was of flowers, measured out a long flower border from our freshwater well to the end of the house that was pleasant to view from the windows. He then erected a three-strand strained wire fence to stop horses and carts from running over the edges. Next he made a similar border stretching from the back door to the privvy, on the left hand side.

My mother loved flowers, and our front window sill was always a riot of colour all the year round. On Wednesdays or Saturdays part of her display had to be moved so she could place a large envelope in the window as a sign for Mr. Fincham, the carrier from Lakenheath, to call. Mother would give him a list of things she needed, and he would purchase them in Bury St. Edmunds and deliver them on his return trip. Mr. Fincham's visit also gave mother, who was a native of Lakenheath, a chance to keep up with Lakenheath news.

When we boys explored the garden, we found the path up the middle had previously been planted with small pear trees on either side. We kept watch on the trees from blossom time until the fruit was ripe, when Dad told us we could have the windfalls. On the left side of the garden, growing up like a high fence, was a row of small fruit trees which produced small round plums, almost white in colour, which Dad said were bullaces; these would ripen to perfection in one day and then drop. Beyond the bullaces stood a wide-spreading apple tree; these apples, he said, were for keeping!

At the very top end of the garden there was a doorway leading to a small meadow. Here he had dug a deep trench to take the daily waste from the pail in the privvy, covering each emptying with a thick layer of fresh soil. He told us that later this would be where the scarlet runner beans would be planted!

In the Autumn we went through the fence and began shaking the bullace trees, because most of the fruit hung on that side. In a few minutes, to our surprise, Freddy Woolard, the church organist, walked up to us carrying a basket and asked if he could share some of the fruit.

Apparently he used to have an allotment that side and Mrs. Woolard was very fond of bullaces. Dad was very pleased to give him a good basketful. Whilst we were that side of the fence we found another well, complete with frame and roller, but obviously disused. We put a temporary cover over it for safety.

When I was quite small my mother took me to St. James's church to attend a wedding of an Icklingham couple. I sat quietly between my mother and another lady, Mrs. George Partridge, from the Sands. As the service drew to its close, I heard the Rector say, 'I now pronounce thee man and wife', whereupon the lady sitting next to me leaned across and said to my mother, 'Her chains are hung on!'

The church stood opposite our house at the other side of the Street. Access was through a gate and along a straight path to an open porch over a sturdy single door. A heavy curtain hung inside to help exclude draughts in winter.

I recall that on some special Sundays our Rector, the Venerable Archdeacon Cartwright, would exchange pulpits with the Rector of Hengrave, who was a wonderful preacher. He would read a text, put down his book, lean over the side of the pulpit and recount some lovely stories. The congregation were entranced; they all agreed they could have listened to him for hours.

In 1911 the church was re-roofed with lead supplied by Lord

Iveagh; the stone parapets were also covered. The work was carried out by Mr. A.G. Budden, the estate plumber, and the lead sheeting was stored in the small barn at the back of our house in the Game Department yard.

Arthur was still living at home and Mr. Budden asked for his help to prepare the lead ready for use. Arthur had to pull on a cord attached to a specially shaped cutting tool which was pulled along the length of the sheets. This operation was repeated until the knife went deep enough to sever the sheet.

A few years later Mr. Budden asked Arthur to join him as 'mate', and he subsequently carried out a considerable amount of deep well work on the estate.

As time went on my mother needed help with the household duties. Dad managed to acquire help from an elderly lady called Mrs. Wiseman, who had two sons, Jesse and John, and a daughter-in-law, Mary Ann.

Mrs. Wiseman,a kindly lady, had a broad Suffolk accent. She was sitting chatting to my mother over a cup of cocoa one day when the talk turned to the subject of vegetable marrows. Mrs. Wiseman suddenly said, in broad Suffolk, 'Mar'ann ha' got some maarster grut uns!'

A mental picture of her buxom daughter-in-law, who walked with her large feet at right-angles, flashed into my head. Before mother could reply, I started to giggle and blurted out, 'What, feet?' Tears began to fill Mrs. Wiseman's eyes. Full of remorse and endeavouring to control my laughter, I said 'Oh! I am so sorry!', whereupon Mrs. Wiseman replied, 'Where's yer sorrer?' This set me off again, and I was sent from the room in disgrace.

A few weeks after our arrival at Icklingham, Mr. William Linney, the farm foreman, came into our yard and told Dad he thought he had located a horse that would be suitable for use by the Game Department. Dad looked the horse over, and Mr. Linney said, 'Shall we try it now?'

Dad said he would not be ready for half an hour. 'Well,' said Mr. Linney, 'make sure someone is holding the horse's head before you get into the cart.' Dad had a quick breakfast, then asked me to help him to harness the horse and get it between the shafts. That done, Dad said, 'Hold the horse's head.' He then put one foot on the cart step and gathered the reins.

He was halfway into the cart when the creature reared, nearly landing on me and making me jump out of the way. The horse bolted out of the yard, turned left, and as it did so I glimpsed my father lying in the bottom of the cart.

I ran to the yard door and was just in time to see the seat fly out of the back. My father was attempting to sit on the side of the cart; fortunately he had the reins in his hands and managed to regain control. Mr. Linney came out of the Church Farm gate, picked up the seat and came over to me. I told him what had happened.

We waited, wondering how long Dad would be. After a while we could hear and then see the horse and cart approaching at a trot, my dad in full control. He told us the horse had soon slackened its pace, but he had forced it to continue at full speed to teach it a lesson.

Mr. Linney suggested another trip. This time, I noticed, he held the horse's head very firmly, which I was too small to do, while my dad climbed back into the cart. This trip proved uneventful, but the Game Department did not purchase the horse!

Dad was lucky that time; some people were not so lucky. One day we heard of a fatal mishap to a horseman, Mr. Walter Ranns from Canada Farm, who had been to Icklingham with a loaded wagon. On his homeward journey he fell over the side of his wagon and a wheel went over his head. His horses continued and returned to their farmyard. The foreman, Mr. Edgar Wright, and another man retraced the wagon's route until they came on the unfortunate man's body. They took him back to his home.

Not long after this sad event my sister May, who had been playing outside, rushed into our kitchen where Dad and I were having dinner. In a distraught manner she whispered into father's ear, 'Colin Linney has been drowned.' Dad leapt to his feet with the words 'Good God!', grabbed his hat and ran out of the house. Maggie told me that it had happened near the water mill.

Colin was the son of the farm bailiff, Mr. William Linney, and was my school chum; we had spent many happy days together. When Dad came back he told us that Jack Gain, who lodged with Carl Marston, the miller, and his wife, had dived repeatedly but in the muddy water could not see Colin's body. Eventually the boy's body was recovered, but too late for artificial respiration to be successful.

The happiest days of your life? 3

HAVING arrived in Icklingham at the age of eight, I was faced with a change of school. My brother Russell took me to Icklingham School for the first time and handed me into the care of a tall girl named Milly Hurrell, who led me into the Infants' Room, situated behind the large room used for the older children.

I had learnt a little at Eriswell School, but I had been absent quite a bit through illness. That first day at the new school I was given a slate and chalk in order to make noughts and crosses, then afterwards I had an interesting session on an abacus; I found the colours on it fascinating. So my first day at Icklingham school made me quite ready to go again the next day.

The small, young teacher in the Infants' Room was Miss Thorpe, who was very kind to her pupils and very well liked by them all.

Two years later, by which time I had moved into the large room, we saw the Ven. A.B. Cartwright come into the school. He told the children that Miss Thorpe was leaving to be married, and as she was so popular with all the children neither he nor they could possibly let her go for any other reason. He presented Miss Thorpe with a wedding gift from the staff and schoolchildren. Miss Thorpe married a young man named Ernest Fordham whose large carrier vehicle, with two horses, passed through Icklingham on Wednesdays and Saturdays on its way from Mildenhall to Bury St. Edmunds. The new Mrs Fordham would often be seen waving to the children as she and her husband passed through the village on the carrier's cart.

The headmistress, Mrs. Mary Woolard, was in charge of the big room. I used to sit next to Gerald Dorling, a gamekeeper's son, who was twice as quick at sums as I was! He was also the messiest at his work, with ink blots on his book and inkstains on his fingers.

Singing lessons were part of our curriculum, and these I enjoyed, but one day something amused me and made me laugh. I had a theory that if you allowed yourself to keep laughing, it would stop quicker. Alas, Mrs. Woolard did not agree. She stopped the singing and said, 'Little boys who can sing, but won't sing, must be made to sing!' I felt this was an injustice, and as she walked away I stuck my tongue out as far as I could. Suddenly she turned round and saw me, I was so surprised that I could not withdraw my tongue. I was immediately sent into a corner of the room and told to stand with my hands held above my head.

Fate, however, was on my side. The tall figure of the Rector was seen approaching the school for his weekly visit, and Mrs Woolard called me back to my place so the visitor should not see me 'standing out'.

On another occasion, the class had to practice a song from another country in Great Britain, and the Scottish 'Auld Lang Syne' was chosen. Mrs Woolard took great pains to explain to us what some of the Scots words in the song meant. 'We twa ha' paidled in the burn, from morning sun till dine, but seas between us braid ha' roared, Sin' Auld Lang Syne'. We were told that a 'burn' was a brook and 'braid' meant broad, and time after time we practised the accent. We did so well that when the inspector came he remarked how well we sang, and with what an excellent 'Scottish' accent!

When I was about nine, Dad asked me one Saturday morning if I would like to go to Elveden with him. I said 'Yes' and clambered into the cart. Off we went up the new private road past Canada Farm and on to Gibson's Lodge, where we joined the Turnpike (what we now call the A11). Soon we were overtaken by a faster horse pulling a lighter cart, Dad keeping to the left to allow him to pass. Dad told me the driver was Mr. Heywood, from Eriswell, who was going to collect the wages from Elveden, just as we were. When we were on the brow of the hill, close to Chalk Hall Farm, Dad pointed out to me the top of the Elveden water tower, situated in the Park, with a very tall tree to its right, which we thought was a spruce.

Arriving at the Game Yard, Dad left me sitting in the cart not far from where a man was busy scrubbing out the stable. He was singing in a deep, musical voice as he worked. He stopped working when he saw me and spoke kindly to me. Dad told me afterwards that the man was Mr. William Alderton, the head keeper's groom. Many years later he was to become my father-in-law.

On the return journey, after we had passed the Crossroads and started up the Chalk Hall hill, Dad had to slow the pony to a walk. Some experiments with road surfacing with hot tar were taking place. First we crossed a strip about six yards wide, then there was a gap, and then another six yards covered with a different type of tar. The work was being carried out by the Estate Works Department, presumably to see which surface was best. At that time the road, maintained by Lord Iveagh from Elveden to Mildenhall and also from Elveden to Brandon, was smooth and level hard-packed sand, stone and chalk.

Even more exciting than that trip to Elveden was the annual Harvest Home outing to Yarmouth each September. I remember going on one of these trips to Yarmouth about 1911, when I was nine or ten, and I particularly recall the build-up of excitement as the great day came when everyone was issued with tickets for the outing.

This particular year Dad decided to drive to Thetford station. We had already been awake for some hours in joyful anticipation when the time came to start, even if we did have to start out quite early in order to catch the train, Dad, Mother, May and Doll in the front seat, Arthur, Russell and I on some straw in the back of the cart.

We made steady progress until we passed through Elveden, then Dad slowed our horse to a walk down Redneck Hill and up the other side, to give it a breather. We reached Thetford station in time for Dad to stable the horse at the Railway Tavern and to exchange our Elveden Estate vouchers for tickets at the ticket office. When the excursion train from Brandon pulled into the station in a cloud of steam Arthur took my hand and I, frightened, buried my face in his coat.

What interesting names the stations had, set out in white lettering on blue boards. Harling Road, Eccles Road, Attleborough, Spooner

Row and Wymondham, Hethersett; and then we reached Norwich Thorpe, where we had to wait for some time. While we waited we watched coal being loaded with a conveyor belt on to the railway trucks of a goods train.

At last we were on our way, excitement mounting as we neared Yarmouth. Dad's plan was to take the steamboat down the river; this way he could keep an eye on us and there was plenty of shipping to look at to occupy our minds, including an extra large vessel unloading timber. Arthur spotted that and called to us to point it out. We all rushed to look over the side. Arthur, who had forgotten he had our one sixpenny piece spending money in his hand, dropped it overboard. We all watched it sink without trace; in deep despair we realized we had lost our day's spending money!

A school group at Icklingham about the time the author attended the school. He is not, however, in the group.

We disembarked at Gorleston and walked to the Aquarium in Yarmouth, where Lord Iveagh's party was due to have lunch. The lunch vouchers were collected, then we awaited the arrival of Lord Iveagh. The Estate agent and Estate Office staff and the Rectors of Elveden, Eriswell and Icklingham were already waiting, seated on a raised platform at the end of the room. Soon His Lordship arrived, accompanied by his private secretary, to be welcomed by one of the Rectors, who said grace. That was a hearty meal — and much appreciated.

After lunch most of the party visited the Hippodrome circus, with its clowns who got us all laughing, the magnificent performing horses, the high wire artists and the acrobats. As if that were not enough, the floor disappeared, then the water rose in the pool below floor level and about twenty swimmers formed graceful patterns on the water.

All too soon the show came to an end and we headed back to the Aquarium, where we surrendered our vouchers for tea. Yarmouth shrimps were in great demand. Tea over, we walked up the well-known Regent Street, where every conceivable item seemed to be available. Dad bought a box of Yarmouth bloaters to take home.

We met up with Joe Bailey, a single man who seldom ventured out of Icklingham. On hearing our tale of woe about our sixpence, Joe gave Arthur a replacement, and also gave my sisters a doll each. We boys were given a bucket and spade and a rubber ball to take home.

By the time we reached Vauxhall Station we were tired and glad to sit with Mother to await the train while
Dad went to the Railway Tavern with Joe. On our way home we heard what had happened in the pub.

On entering the pub, Joe had ordered drinks all round. He had then proceeded to tell a local fisherman that he could catch more rabbits in his net than the fisherman could catch herrings in his! He called for more drinks all round, and continued to bait the fisherman, who at last lost his temper and wanted to fight. It could have been a nasty situation, but his mates grabbed him and told him, 'Don't you touch him, you old fool, he's buying all the beer!'

Once aboard the train, we children slept most of the way back to Thetford. Dad collected the horse and cart from the Station Tavern and we journeyed home.

Dad and Mother agreed that the day's outing had been one of the hardest days they'd ever had!

During my schooldays I witnessed two fistfights between boys. I happened to go back early after dinner one day and noticed two boys in the porch, where we hung up our coats. Both were 'dinner boys', those who stayed at school for dinner. One was 'Ginger' Ward from Avenue Farm and the other George Ranns from Canada Farm, and they were fighting. I noticed how easily George parried Ginger's blows, but regularly landed his own straight from the shoulder. Ginger's nose was bleeding and he was soundly beaten, whilst George appeared unmarked.

The second fight was quite different. It took place in our grass playground, and the combatants were both older boys, Bob Petch and Sid Wiseman. Harry Wiseman acted as 'second' to Bob and Herbert Petch acted for Sid. Little skill was displayed, with many 'haymakers' being thrown. They each sustained blows which caused profuse nose bleeds, whereupon their seconds stopped the fight and made them shake hands. Fortunately a wash-basin and water supply had been installed in the corner of the hard playground, and the boxers were soon washed clean by their seconds. From then on the two boys became friends.

At the bottom of the grass playground, where a lovely wild rose grew, was a fence which separated the playground from the narrow Mill Lane which was regularly used by the miller, Carl Marston. The lane had been 'skirted' to make it slightly wider, the skirtings having been thrown up on to the bank just outside the school fence.

During morning playtime boys ran down to the fence and quickly collected as many of these 'skirtings' as they could. They waited for the miller to come along, and when he was level with them they bombarded him with the clods, which not only spread dirt on his face and neck but also fell on to his bags of meal.

He stopped his horse, jumped on to the bank and over the fence.

Ignoring the smaller boys, he chased the older ones, who by this time had reached the hard ground, caught two of them and banged their heads together. After that he resumed his journey.

Whilst I was still at school it became very fashionable to wear stiff white celluloid collars. The boys soon found out that if the sun's rays were focused with a magnifying glass on to these collars they would go up in flames. After a number of 'accidents' when boys were burnt, the collars were banned.

Peg tops were very popular. A boy armed with his own top and the right length of suitable string could often split another boy's top in half if his aim were accurate. I possessed one which already had a 'shake' in it, and it therefore was a prime target. However, it must have been exceptionally hard, for it was never split. We used to stand in a large circle and had great fun knocking down a 'target' top.

Joe Palmer was very keen on organising our playing at being 'teams of horses'. His father worked on a farm, so there was no problem obtaining binder twine. Boys would join in and drape the twine over their shoulders to form a 'back row'; the twine then reached forward to form the 'front row'. These front row 'horses' had a short piece of clean stick held in their mouths as a 'bit'. Joe would crack his whip and issue commands.

One dinnertime Mrs. Woolard, from inside the schoolroom, heard Joe say 'Come on old mare!' She went into fits of laughter, and told us how she had enjoyed watching; we really had acted like a team of horses, she said.

Growing up 4

DURING my schooldays we used to play plenty of cricket in the 'green' playground. This gave me an idea to make a pitch on our own meadow, where Dad used to turn out our old sow during the day. She was really a family pet, and when we came out of school we used to go to the meadow and sit on top of the gate to see her.

'Sukie', as we used to call her, would come rushing down the meadow to see us, with her big ears flapping. We used to say 'tig, tig, tig' and scratch her back, whereupon she would give a contented grunt and roll over on her side.

I selected what I considered to be the best spot for a pitch, in the middle of the meadow, measured eighteen yards and started to trim the grass with my dad's reap hook. I found that this left some spiky stems sticking up, so I went indoors and quietly borrowed my mother's scissors, which she used to use to trim the lamp wick. On hands and knees I clipped off the spiky bits.

I also 'borrowed' some rabbit net stakes and made them into six wickets, complete with bails. When we played cricket at school, Sam Atkins used to bring a bat which his father had shortened, making it about the right length for boys. On Saturday morning I invited those who were keen to join me and my brothers Arthur and Russell for a 'knock-up'.

As we hadn't a ball, we collected twelve halfpennies from our 'team' and went merrily to the Post Office, where we purchased a bright-red, hard cork ball for sixpence from Mr. George Naylor. Play commenced, and we enjoyed our game until the ball was hit into some undergrowth at the side of the meadow. Try as we would we could not find our new ball.

We then noticed that Sukie was lying down in the undergrowth and something red was showing at the side of her mouth — *our ball!* She then dropped the ball, already half chewed away, and that put an end to our game for that day.

When we told Dad he was very worried because he thought the cork would swell up and cause internal problems, but days passed and Sukie did not appear to have taken any harm. Dad was so relieved that he gave us sixpence to buy a new ball.

Many years later I went from Elveden to Icklingham to play cricket. One of the Petch family, who was scoring, greeted me with the words, 'Do you remember the day when the sow ate the ball?'

Boys from the village and Canada Farm used to join us for a game on Saturdays. Many a time the ball landed on the thatched barn, only to roll down again into the meadow. Only my brother Arthur and Jack Good, a boy from next door, ever managed to hit the ball clean over the barn.

Once Fred Ranns was hit on his thumb, which was squashed between the bat handle and ball; I well remember the big blood blister that quickly formed.

When we were young the highlight of our year was, of course, Christmas. There was a build-up of excitement as preparations proceeded. Making Christmas cakes and puddings for a large family meant many hours of cleaning fruit, with eager hands waiting for titbits. The cakes and puddings could be made well beforehand, but the baking of other things like mince pies was delayed as long as possible, to ensure that they would be nice and fresh on the great day.

My brother Ian usually lived with our grandmother at Eriswell[1], but sometimes Arthur, our eldest brother, would stay with her so that Ian could have a few days at home with us. This was the case on this particular Christmas.

The Farms used our small meadow to rear turkeys. We heard the constant noise they made, especially at feeding times, and were

[1] It was not uncommon in days of large families and restricted accommodation for one of the children to be boarded out with relatives. In this case the reason seems to have been to assist the ageing grandmother; Ian could do some of the routine jobs such as fetching water and cutting sticks, and no doubt his companionship was as valuable as his help.

amazed how quickly they developed. One morning Ian (always pronounced 'iron' by his contemporaries and therefore nicknamed 'Tinny') and I were watching the birds when Tinny picked up a smooth stone and shied it at a large bird. To our horror the stone hit it on its head, and it fell to the ground and lay quite still. We had been told to be careful not to harm the birds, so what explanation could we think of for this tragic event? Ian and I were discussing our best line of approach when to our great joy the bird suddenly stood up; it had only been stunned!

Christmas Eve arrived, and we were washed and sent to bed. My brother Russell was sleeping with me, both of us were quite excited. In the early hours of the morning we heard slow, stealthy footsteps and the sound of the door quietly opening. We pretended to be fast asleep as we heard Mum and Dad attach two long stockings, one for each of us, to the foot of the bed. When they left they took away the candle, and we had to wait until daylight.

Russell soon untied his stocking, which was a large woollen one of Dad's. There was a written note wishing him A Happy Christmas at the top, we could feel oranges in the toe, then figs and dates. Next we unwrapped some toys. I pulled out a bag of sweets, and then came upon a toy cockerel on a strong spring fixed to a small box. When one pressed the cockerel down firmly it crowed loudly.

I demonstrated this to Russell. His only comment was, 'I had that last year!' Each year the toys disappeared after breakfast, and much later we realized that they were being rotated annually between us four boys!

Early on Christmas morning I heard my father lighting a fire in our sitting-room and putting the fireguard in front of it to prevent any stray sparks from flying on to our largest and best carpet, which only covered the central section of the room; a brown painted border covered the rest of the floorboards. Our best oak table was laid ready for the items we should be enjoying for tea, which would include mince pies, nuts, dates, figs, and so on.

For Christmas Dad had received a large sirloin of beef and other goodies for tea from the Estate. Incidentally, on this occasion the butcher was a Mr. G. Lummis from Lakenheath, who had had permission from the Estate Office to use our barn to slaughter the bullock. We boys had a good view of large parts of the carcase as they were hung for the appropriate time before final cutting up for distribution.

Mother cooked the sirloin in the dutch oven. The vegetables were cooked on the Beetonette range in the kitchen, whilst the plum pudding had its final boil in the copper. Our large kitchen table was spread with the best tablecloth and cutlery.

The table was now ready for the repast! My father took his position at the head of the table, touched up the knife with the steel, and then proceeded with the carving. Grace was said, and we all began to eat our Christmas dinner.

At teatime in the sitting-room the best oil lamp, with its special globe, was lit. After tea we played games, and then gathered round the fire to sing hymns and carols. So ended our Christmas Day, and then we children, tired but happy, made our way to bed.

Boys will be boys, they say, and we certainly weren't any exception to that rule. I recall that on one cold moonlit night my brother Russell and Victor Turner lifted all the front gates along the Street from their hinges, starting near Cavenham Lane, and placed them out of sight on the opposite side of the road. Snow had begun to fall, and Russell had just walked through our gate when P.c. Sladden started out on his rounds of the village. Perhaps he noticed the footsteps leading up to our gate, but next day the constable questioned Russell about the gate incident; naturally he denied any knowledge of it.

Another time Russell and Victor were chatting to Prissy Palmer when her father came rushing out waving a poker and saying, 'I'll make you run, you b★★★★★★★!' They ran across the road, leapt a low wall and dashed along a narrow pathway leading to a disused well. They ducked under the frame holding the roller and handle, but in their frantic haste they didn't notice that there was no covering over the well and were fortunate not to fall in!

Soon I was old enough to become a member of the church choir. We boys used to arrive early to put on our black cassocks and white surplices and then sit on a row of chairs near the door. James Pollard, the verger, would stand at the door to open it when he heard footsteps in the porch. At evening service we could smell his breath because he always ate raw onions for tea.

At one Harvest Festival it was so cold that the cast iron stove had been lit to take the chill off the church, and it was glowing red hot. A

The choir of St. James's Church, Icklingham, a photograph taken on 12th June, 1914. In the back row, left to right, are George Dorling, Sam Atkins, Walter Hunt, Arthur Palmer, unknown, Sid Darkins, Bill Linney and Ernie Linney. In the middle row are Herbert Petch, Archibald Rainbird, Tommy Atkins, Freddie Woolard (the organist), Bill Partridge, George Partridge, Russell Turner, Barry Kybird and Harry Bailey (postman and gravedigger). Standing just in front of the middle row at right is Carl Marston. Seated in front are Colin Linney, the author, the Ven. Arthur Babylon Cartwright, Bob Petch and Henry (Frisky) Petch.

tall young man entered and as he passed the stove he surreptitiously sprinkled some tobacco on to the top, then proceeded to a pew on the left of the aisle. As the choir processed to the choir stalls an acrid smell pervaded the church, causing much coughing amongst the congregation, whilst they sang the first harvest hymn.

Later that year the choir practised a hymn in which the trebles had to sing the verse which begins 'The golden evening brightens in the West', unaccompanied. I was so worried about this that I did not sleep the previous night. On the Sunday my nerves were still taut, but when the moment came to sing I found I was managing quite comfortably with the other boys.

In the vestry afterwards, one of the choristers named Tommy Atkins took me aside and said, 'Ted, you have a good, strong voice, but you do not open your mouth wide enough.' Good advice, which the organist had never given me. One of his sayings which would always amuse us was, 'Put the haccent on that hef!'

The following Christmastide I went with a party of carol singers, led by Mr. Thomas Atkins. The starting point was The Bell, a pub in West Street, whose landlord, Mr. Arthur Payne, kindly let the boys sit in a shelter just outside the back door, where his wife supplied us with lemonade and ginger beer. The men seemed to spend rather a long time inside, but eventually we proceeded on our way.

I remember Dad and Mother standing at their front door to hear the carols. When we arrived at the Hall, Doctor and Mrs. Sturge listened to a few carols at their front door, then we trooped to the side door in the yard to sing to the staff. Before long we arrived at the Red Lion, where the men went inside and once again we boys seemed to wait an extra long time outside.

The men refreshed, we visited more cottages, the Post Office and Flint House. With 'Happy Christmas' ringing in our ears, we carried on to The Plough for more refreshment, then down and up the hill to The Crown and even more refreshment, finally finishing at Mitchell's Farm. Wearily we trudged back to the Rectory, where the Ven. Archdeacon Cartwright and his wife greeted us. Whilst the collecting boxes were being emptied and the contents counted, the staff served us with hot mincepies, for which we very grateful. The result of our efforts was announced at church on Christmas Day.

Just after Christmas the choir were invited to the annual supper at the Rectory. Earlier that year, Dad's cousin who lived in London had sent us a very nice blue velvet 'Little Lord Fauntleroy' style jacket, which unfortunately happened to fit me and which my mother insisted I must wear when I went to the choir supper.

We were shown into the Rectory dining room and sat down at the large table which was already laid for us. The Archdeacon sat down at the head of the table, and then staff brought in a large quantity of delicious food, to which we all did full justice. When we came to the plum pudding the host tried to ignite the brandy, but failed after two or three attempts. Crackers were pulled, and a spark flew into my right eye, which began to water copiously. The Archdeacon expressed his appreciation to his staff, who had prepared the supper, to which we all said 'Hear! Hear!' and clapped.

After this Mr. Cartwright took us outside to the edge of the sunken lawn and produced some strips of white material, which when he ignited them burned brilliantly and illuminated the entire lawn with a white light. I later discovered these were strips of magnesium used for photography at that time.

Suddenly someone said they could smell something burning. On inspection it was found to be the front of my velvet jacket, which was smouldering and totally ruined. Back we all went to the warm dining room, where some of the men sang their party pieces. Tommy Atkins sang 'Sons of the Sea', Bill Partridge contributed 'When Father Painted the Parlour', and so the evening came to a close. We thanked our hosts and wished them a Happy New Year, then left for home.

When Russell and I arrived home we had to show Dad and Mum what had happened to their treasured little blue coat. They were both very upset. I ought not to say it, but I was overjoyed as I disliked it intensely!

Dr. Allen and Mrs. Sturge, of Icklingham Hall, spent much of their retirement walking over the sandy parts of Icklingham in search of flint implements, for which the area was noted. They had regular evenings each week when parishioners would bring 'worked' flints to the Hall for them to inspect. Many fine arrowheads and other flints were taken to them and a fair price was paid for each one, this to men whose weekly wage was never more than ten shillings. Even a selection of unworked flints would earn the collector a small sum for bringing them in, and the gardeners would subsequently take these to the top of the Hall grounds and place them in ruts along the 'backway'. One Sunday morning, Dad went out early and saw a man named Ernie picking up some of these flints. Dad told him that those flints had already been discarded, receiving the reply that Dr. Sturge wouldn't know he had seen them before and he would give him two shillings for bringing them in!

Dr. Sturge was proud to show Dad the splendid collection he had assembled, all neatly labelled with the relevant information as to their uses, arrowheads, axe heads, knives and so on. Dad was very interested and made a good collection himself; some items were dug out by warreners when digging for rabbits, he always paid them for their trouble.

During the Harvest Holidays Dr. and Mrs. Sturge encouraged the schoolchildren to collect as many wild flowers as they could find and take them in with a list of the names of those that they knew. They were allowed to use local names. Some children would collect over a hundred flowers, and it took quite a time to sort them out. Every child received some small reward for their effort.

Usually my bunch was quite small, but one year Dad told me where I could find a poisonous Henbane, a repulsive- looking flower. He said I should be very careful how I handled it! I went to the foot of the large tree where he had seen it, and there it was. The spot was near a large enclosure known as the 'Ancient Roman Camp', not far from Temple Bridge over the River Lark.

When I took my bunch of flowers to The Hall I was quite excited. When Doctor Sturge noticed the name 'henbane' on my list and saw the flower, he said he was not aware that they grew in the area at all. He was so pleased he gave me a half-crown, I was delighted! The following year my dad and I watched the foot of the same tree, but we never saw another plant. Presumably a bird had brought that solitary seed.

During 1910 Arthur and I both contracted Scarlet Fever, which was prevalent in the village. The precautions taken to prevent the spread of the illness to other members of the family were to hang a sheet soaked in disinfectant over the doorway and to keep a window open.

After a few days of high temperature our chests and backs began to peel. This dry, infectious skin had to be removed from the sheets and placed in a bag to be burnt.

Fortunately, Arthur's was a mild attack, and after a number of days the doctor allowed him to get up. Mine was more severe, and I had to have a further week in bed, then another spell confined to the bedroom but allowed to dress and sit looking out of the window.

In due time I was allowed to go downstairs. Then I decided to take a short walk in the March sun. It was just as well I took a stick to steady me, for to my surprise the ground seemed to come up and meet each step. I also found that cow parsley had sprung up, which made walking even more difficult. After a time I realized it was all due to the muscles having become weak after having been inactive for so long.

In 1911 my father realized that he had an awful sore throat. He had to consult the doctor from Mildenhall, who diagnosed the dreaded diphtheria. This was reported to the Estate Office, and Lord Iveagh gave immediate instructions for a trained nurse from the Queen Alexandra's School of Nursing to be sent at once. Mother put our sitting-room at her disposal for use as a bedroom, because the nurse would have to sleep in the daytime after staying up to watch Dad all night.

The nurse, Sister Dora Braithwaite, arrived in Lord Iveagh's own car, driven by a chauffeur who knew exactly where our house, No. 24, was. Mother told us we must keep quiet, day and night, for the sake of my father and Sister Dora.

The doctor kept in direct touch with Lord Iveagh, and when after a few days Dad could hardly breathe, Lord Iveagh sent his car to Cambridge to fetch vital medication from the Lister Institute of Preventive Medicine. Once the doctor had administered it the effect was miraculous; within a few minutes the swelling in Dad's throat began to subside and he could breathe easily once more, no longer with short painful gasps.

With the crisis past, Sister Dora was able to rebuild his strength gradually. During the day, when Sister Dora had had her rest time, she would take Dad's favourite retriever bitch, also named Dora, down the meadow and along the river bank to exercise and take the air. When she returned she would help Mother to get our tea ready for when we came out of school.

One thing she demonstrated was making scrambled eggs; we kids loved it as it was something new. We all called her 'Sister', and she soon became familiar with our christian names. She taught us a song to sing with her:

> Oh poor Margot, went for a row,
> She fell right into the river, cruel river, Oh, oh, oh!
> Three nice young men came by, she cried out, Hi,hi, hi,
> I'm drowning in the river, cruel river! Oh,oh,oh,
> The three jumped in and said,
> We'll save you from the river, cruel river, oh,oh,oh!

When we had become accustomed to the words, Sister Dora patiently spent time while we practised singing whilst Mother listened. Suddenly she looked at me and nodded to Mother; 'He's got it,' she said. They were both very pleased.

After a few more weeks Dad was able to take short walks up the meadow and along the back-way. One bright morning he set off with his walking stick and continued further than usual. He was some way from home when weakness seized him, he turned back but felt so bad he did not think he would ever reach home.

Sister Dora knew he had been away longer than usual, and was waiting at the door to help him in. She gave him two tots of whisky, and made him lie on the bed in order to massage his legs. Dad told me afterwards he was certain she had saved his life a second time!

From then on he made good progress. The time came when we all had to say goodbye to Sister Dora, who had been such a good friend to us all.

About this time I had been having instruction to prepare me for confirmation. The Icklingham candidates had to attend Mildenhall Church, where the Bishop of Ely would carry out the laying on of hands. The youngest candidates, me among them, travelled in Mr. Linney's horse and cart. After the service we had strawberries from the Rector's garden and cream, served in the church room.

Then I walked the short distance to the High Street, where to my surprise I met my brother Russell. He was ready to return home, so I said I would rather ride back on his bicycle step than be cooped up in the cart with the others. Off we went and stayed ahead of the horse and cart until we went down the short hill opposite Avenue Drift, where my foot slipped off the step and I fell on my face just as the cart, full of youngsters roaring with glee, passed by. Thankfully, I was not badly hurt; only my pride suffered.

Time passed, and I had already been granted permission to leave school at the age of thirteen. As my birthday drew near I sensed something was afoot, little incidents or snide remarks would crop up. My very last day came and we were all dismissed.

As we filed out I made a dash for the bottom of the green playground and backed into the corner with both fists clenched. The pack came rushing after me. I said, 'The first one near me will get my fist on his nose!' They all hesitated, and gradually moved away. Whatever their plan had been, they realized that they could not carry it out as easily as they had hoped!

The village of Icklingham 5

WHEN I was a lad the village of Icklingham was a rather different place from what it is now. Of course everyone knew everyone else, where they lived, and what they did; sometimes, perhaps, we knew more than was good for us about some of the other residents, and often they knew more about us than was good for us, but that goes with living in a village of little more than three hundred souls.

'Icklingham is a township, comprising the parishes of St. James and All Saints, which are united for civil purposes and form one village,' so Kelly's *Directory of Suffolk* (1916 edition) tells us. 'The village, about a mile in length, stands on the north bank of the river Lark . . .'.

There follows a lengthy note about the two churches standing less than half a mile apart, about the memorials in the churches, and so on. 'Alice Dix's charity is applied to the maintenance of a dispensary, the provision of clothing for the poor and the support of the National School. It is now under the control of a body consisting of the rector (ex-officio) and four elected trustees with two others appointed by the Parish Council. A Roman encampment once existed on the eastern side of the village, and numerous coins, urns and other antiquities have been found on this spot, including about 200 silver coins of various Roman Emperors, turned up at different times by the plough . . . the chief crops are wheat, barley and turnips.'

Well, that is the outsider looking in; what was the village like as we saw it? Come with me for a walk, and I'll show you.

We'll start right at the west end of the village, down West Street. At the far end of West Street lay the area called The Sands; as its name implies, it was the junction of West Street with the sandy warren land that stretched out towards Temple Bridge spanning the Lark. I have been told that the bridge derived its name from the body of Knights Templar who had a mission there to assist travellers on their journey.

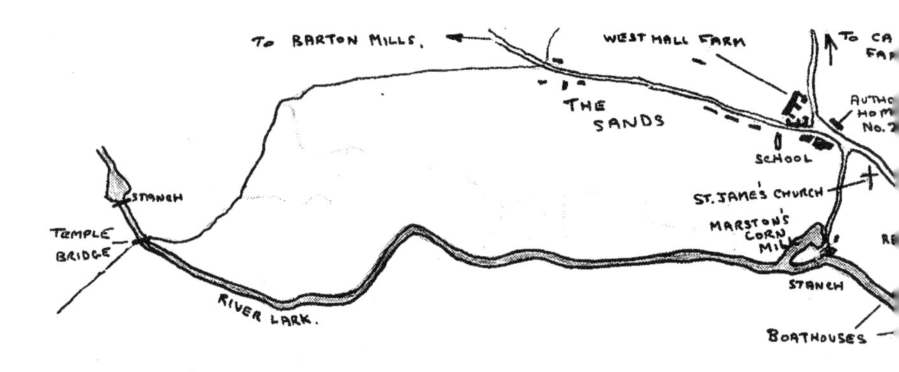

NOTE. METHODIST CHAPEL AS SHOWN ON THIS MAP LATER REPLACED BY A NEW ONE ON OTHER SIDE OF ROAD. ALSO WESTHALL FARM RENAMED HOME FARM

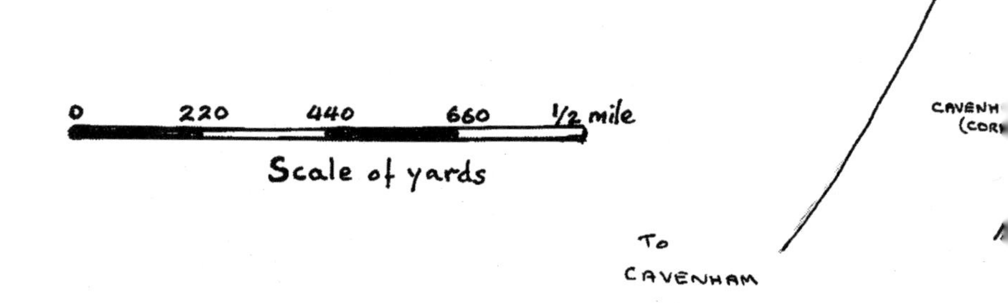

Sketch map of Icklingham

as remembered by Edward Turner

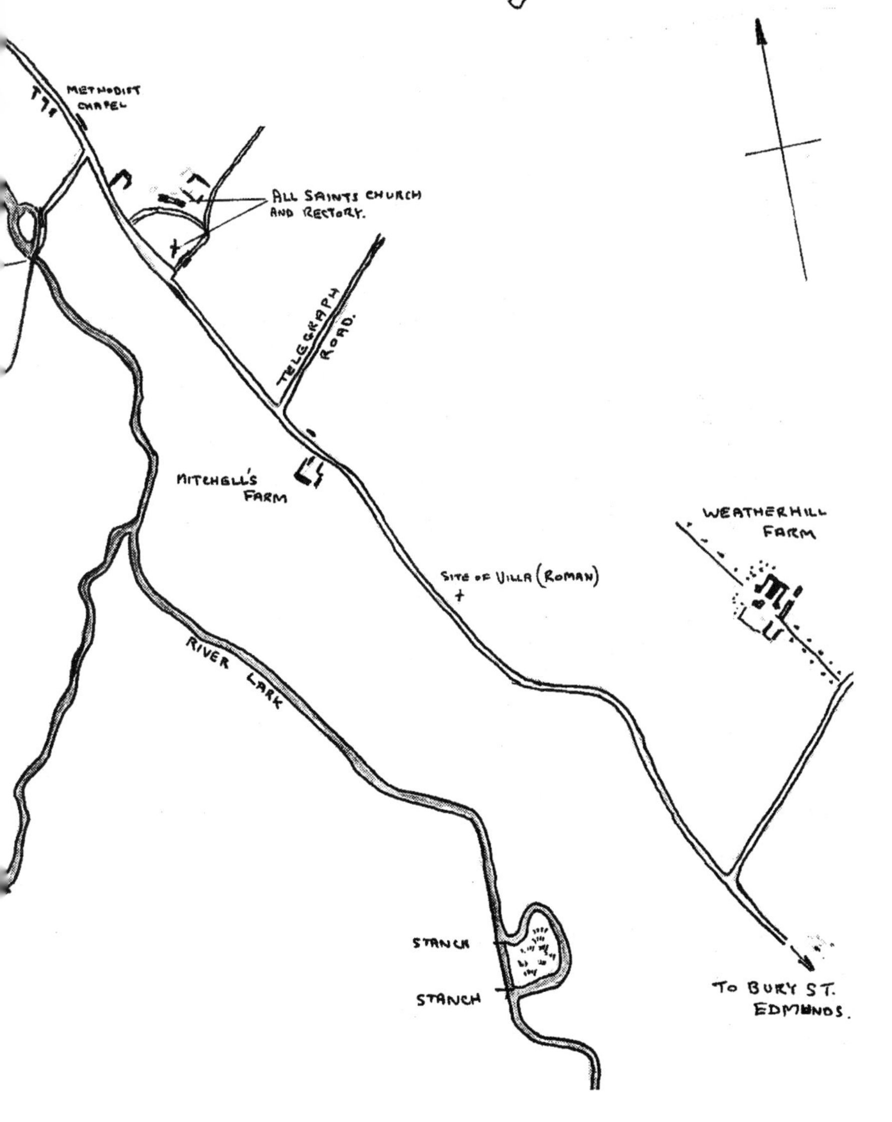

Looking east, on the right was a small thatched cottage lived in by a retired farmworker named Jarrold and his wife. They were the parents of George and Charles Jarrold and of Mrs. David Wright (see the wedding photograph on page 95).

Two more thatched dwellings were close by, one occupied by Miss Nancy Ward and her two lodgers, Jerry Went, a farmworker at Avenue Farm, and Philip Brunning. Miss Ward had spent her life working on the land, and as a result of her work in the fields her back was extremely bent; people would say as she went past, 'There go old Nance, her head's at Mitchell's Farm and her arse at the Sands'.

The next large thatched house was in disrepair and unoccupied. The occupant of the first house on the left was Ted Fletcher, a carpenter employed at the Icklingham Clerk of Works department, and the next house sheltered the Sharman family. Then came a new house built for Mr. Horrocks, the retired butler from Icklingham Hall.

Passing a meadow, one came on some quoit beds where matches against neighbouring parishes were keenly contested. Quoits, in which the players throw a steel ring or quoit towards a clay bed, has not quite died out in Suffolk yet, and there are still places you can see it played. Behind the quoit beds was a bungalow where a ploughman, Frank Childerstone, lived with his family, and nearby was another small house standing in its own garden adjoining the cricket meadow; the tenant was Miss M. Brunning, a retired housemaid.

Moving east, there were two cottages on the right, then another two occupied by the Levett family, farmworkers at Avenue Farm, and a single man named Collins, who also worked on one of the farms. The next thatched house stood end-on to the road, and at the far end of the house was a spring supplying pure drinking water, one of a number constantly bubbling to the surface and nourishing a steady supply of watercress. Mrs. Darkins, a widow, lived there.

The village constable, P.c. Gooderham, lived in the next house; he was later succeeded by P.c. Edward Sladden. Next one came to the church school, of which Mrs. M.A. Woolard was the headmistress; her husband Frederick was the church organist.

Still on the left, where West Street joined the main village street, was situated the Church Farmhouse, with extensive buildings and stackyard. Behind these lay the meadow used as a cricket ground, always a place of great interest to me. On the right nearly opposite the two quoit beds were two small houses, one occupied by William Partridge, who delivered coal for Mr. Naylor, the Postmaster, then the little public house called The Bell, the publican being Arthur Payne. Still moving east, one came on the right to the narrow lane leading to the noisy water mill on the Lark; the miller was Carl Marston.

Next one comes to St. James's Church, with the churchyard wall along the edge of the road. Opposite the church stands the Gamekeeper's thatched house, where I lived with my parents from March, 1909, to January, 1919. The next house was occupied by the maltster, named Hartwell, who worked in the maltings near the Red Lion.

Further on was Icklingham Hall, with its extensive lawns and attractive gardens behind a high wall with ornamental iron gates. Opposite, running parallel with the road, were ornamental chains and a sunken ha ha wall before a meadow which led down to the river.

Beyond were some delightful spring gardens with rustic bridges and bubbling springs. The Hall laundry and chauffeur's house were also opposite the Hall; Mr. Rainbird was the chauffeur. Next one came to the maltings, where Mr. Hartwell worked before the war; early in the war the building was used as an army mess.

Here, well back from the road, stood the Red Lion Inn, which had been stripped of its thatch and re-roofed with corrugated iron, much to the disgust of the local thatcher, Mr. Grainger. This inn was a favourite pull-in for farmers and others returning from Bury market on Wednesdays, when village boys would vie with each other to hold the horses in return for a small coin.

Then came a cottage where a boot and shoe repairer lived for a time. On to the Dispensary, where a nurse lived with her companion who owned a pony and governess cart, the kind that had a door and a step at the back. Surgery was held once a week by a Dr. Glasier from Mildenhall. The parish should have been particularly well served for medical care during the period just prior to 1914, because as well as the weekly surgery and the resident district nurse at the dispensary the Rector had studied medicine before taking Holy Orders. The doctor had been heard to comment 'Damn the Parson, let him stick to his text!' In addition, the residents at the Hall, Mr. and Mrs. Allen Sturge, were a retired surgeon and a former hospital matron. Surely enough know-how there to provide the best for the sick and needy.

Next to Icklingham Hall was a thatched house used as a small shop, where Alfred Frost lived with his sister. Some land and an orchard were part of the property, and pigs were bred and reared there. Schoolboys, who should have known better, used to queue outside the shop, entering one at a time at intervals just long enough for the kindly Miss Frost to get back into her kitchen before she was disturbed yet again to take a paltry sum for a small purchase.

Still following the village street, one came to the thatched double dwelling occupied by the Hurrell and Palmer families. The former possessed a magnificent mulberry tree which annually seemed to produce enough fruit to supply the whole village population. Mr. Hurrell was a former regular soldier; Fred Palmer worked on Home

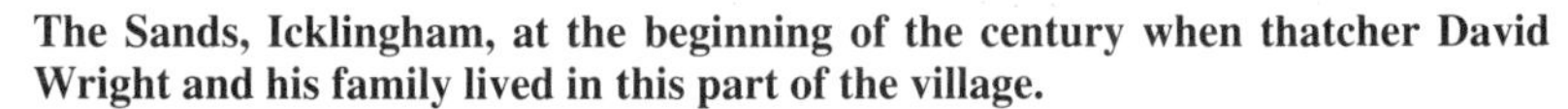
The Sands, Icklingham, at the beginning of the century when thatcher David Wright and his family lived in this part of the village.

Farm, or Westhall Farm as it was known in the Maharajah's day.

The village Post Office and General Stores came next, the postmaster being Mr. George Naylor. Every conceivable item could be obtained there, and coal and paraffin were distributed weekly from the stores. Opposite the Post Office stood a somewhat dilapidated thatched building which served as a storehouse. Next door was a thatched house occupied by a Mr. Leverton, a retired man. Here a footpath at right angles to the street led to the Postman's hut, used daily by the postman delivering the Royal Mail from Mildenhall. The path entrance was marked by a large beech tree standing on the boundary between the parishes of All Saints and St. James.

The more modern building opposite the beech tree was appropriately named Flint House and was lived in by the Rudling and Atkins families. Behind it lay the Estate carpenters' shop, where Mr. Rudling worked. Tommy Atkins was a bricklayer, also working for the Clerk of Works.

Passing another house occupied by the Wright and Rayner families, we come to the Methodist Chapel. Mr. David Wright was a thatcher, and in later years Mrs. Wright came to help my mother when she became ill with tuberculosis. Mr. and Mrs. Rayner both worked at Canada Farm.

Just to the west and in close proximity to the chapel was a spacious building with a corrugated roof which served as a Reading Room, a dance hall and a place for afternoon religious services when blackout restrictions during the war curtailed the use of the churches.

Almost opposite the chapel was a bungalow occupied by the Bailey family. The next house was occupied by Mr. R. Levett, and the next by Miss Hood. Both Bailey and Levett were warreners. At right angles a green road led through Roan Hall stackyard and beyond to Belle Vue. Opposite this green road lay the Cavenham Lane, leading to the three bridges over the Lark and so to Cavenham.

Back to the village street, heading east we come to a cluster of small houses called Bolton's Yard, where families named Grainger, Fuller, Petch and Warren lived. Next came Roan Hall, with occupants Stevens and Turner; adjoining were extensive farm premises with the traditional barn.

Lying well back from the road and approached by a gravel drive was the Rectory, occupied by the Ven. Archdeacon A.B. Cartwright. Looking from the Rectory, but slightly to the left, the square tower of the ancient church of All Saints could be observed with its roof of thatch.

Beyond the church comes the Church Lane, leading to the Pilgrim's Path, said to have been a path used in the Middle Ages by pilgrims on their way to the shrine at Walsingham. In Church Lane one found a cottage occupied by the Rectory gardener, James Pollard, who also carried out the duties of Church Clerk at St. James's Church.

Across the road, opposite the church, stood a cottage rented by Mrs. Cornell as well as the forge, operated by Robert Harding, and the blacksmith's cottage. Still moving east, a few cottages preceded the Plough Inn, whose landlord, Mr. George Fitches, also bred pigs, but never allowed a single loose straw to be seen in his yard.

Re-crossing the street, we go downhill to the next thatched cottage, where William Macro lived with his mother and sister. As in a number of Icklingham houses, the front doorstep obstructed the path and protruded into the roadway.

Moving to the bottom of the hill, the next building was used as a shop, the owner at one time being Mr. Cracknell. Next came a row of small houses, one being occupied by Harry Cornish, a warrener.

Across the width of Telegraph Road[1], a cart track, stands Jubilee Cottage, tenanted by Will Hunt, a warrener employed on the Culford Estate. This cottage stands on the corner of Wing's Field, on which Wing's Barn is also situated. A short distance along Telegraph Road there was a small cottage, the home of Jack Cornish, a warrener.

Retracing our steps, we emerge from Telegraph Road to cross the street to The Crown public house, where the landlord, Mr. James Crocombe, used to act as loader for guests on the Elveden Estate shoots. He had at one time been valet to Sir Evelyn Wood.

[1] Telegraph Road was named after the Admiralty telegraph station that stood at the top of the lane in Napoleonic times. It was one of a chain of such stations linking London with Yarmouth.

Still continuing eastwards, we move uphill to Mitchell's Farm, with its large barn and outbuildings. Nearly opposite there is a small bungalow, the home of Harry Bailey, who combined the jobs of postman and parish gravedigger. The road continues with a series of curves for a considerable distance to reach the Lackford boundary, where stands the house occupied by the Nichols family. Lying well back from the road was the property known as Weatherhill Farm, rented by a Mr. Harry Smith, who subsequently moved to the Ingham Griffin pub. His horsekeeper, who lived nearby, was Jack Boughen.

We now retrace our steps through the village past the shop, the pubs and the two churches to the point where the road turns right. Following this a short distance, we see the entrance to the 'New Road' or private drive, with its heavy white gate. The modern gatehouse, a double dwelling, was occupied by the retired schoolmaster, Mr. J. Forby-Smith, and his family and a Mrs. Wright and her family.

Continuing along the drive for about two miles we come to Canada Farm, where the foreman, Edgar Wright, and his family lived, together with the horsekeeper, Walter Ranns, and his family and also Michael Brunning, the shepherd.

A field on Canada Farm was chosen as the first place where sugar beet was grown on the Elveden Estate. Leaving Canada Farm, we go east to Bernersfields, where a gamekeeper, William Dorling, lived with his family. His neighbour was Jack Hazelwood, a farmworker. Bernersfields was chosen as an experimental site for tobacco growing.

Returning to the gatehouse, we turn west on the Eriswell Road for a mile, which brings us to Avenue Farm. The foreman there was John Wiseman, who lived there with his family. The horseman, Alfred Ward, and his family also lived at Avenue Farm. Moving down the Avenue Drift towards the Mildenhall Road we come to the cottage where a horsekeeper named Dorling lived beside gamekeeper James Dorling and his family. Though they shared the same surname, the two neighbours were not related.

That was the village in which I grew up, and those were the people who were our neighbours.

Work experience 6

SOME time before I left school Mr. Grainger, the house thatcher, asked my dad if I could join him after school, at 4 p.m., and spend an hour 'threading the needle'. Dad agreed, so I joined Mr. Grainger that afternoon.

Alan Linney came out of school at the same time, and as soon as he saw me he began to chant 'bunch, broaches, tar-line, bottels', much to my annoyance; those are thatching tools and materials.

My job was to remove the tarred cord from the big iron needle, pass it round the rafter and thread the needle again as Mr. Grainger pushed it through on the other side. I mounted the granary steps and took up my position on a cross-beam, balancing myself by gripping the underside of a rafter. The thatcher, out of sight on the thatch above me, shouted, 'Are you ready?' 'Yes!' I said, and work began.

After a few needles had been threaded, an extra powerful thrust came through the thatch. I yelled with pain, as one of my fingers had been pierced. 'What did I get you, mate?' 'Yes!' I said, realizing I had foolishly let my finger get too far above the rafter. 'I think we can have a few minutes rest,' said Mr. Grainger, knowing how bad I felt. After this he sent me home early, but I reported back for work the next day and continued until the job was done, with no further mishaps. I received my sixpences.

I attained the age of thirteen on 21st October, 1915, and was then given a special certificate allowing me to leave Icklingham C.P. School a year earlier than usual in order to assist with any necessary work on the land. The Great War had by then raged for over a year and thousands of men had joined the Forces, leaving the home front very short of manpower.

With winter at hand I was supplied with a number of mole traps and was primarily engaged in setting these over a large area and visiting them every day, with varying success. Many crafty moles would either go under or around the trap, or go up to it and turn back. I gradually learned some of the tricks of the trade, and in due course accumulated a number of skins. I eagerly awaited the return of my first postal order from the skin merchant, but suffered an anti-climax when I received about half the expected value, with the information that I had dried the skins in the wrong shape! This very first income was taken upstairs to my mother, who was ill in bed. 'Now I can get you a new pair of breeches, which you so badly need,' she told me.

In February, 1916, there was a heavy snowfall and I was unable to visit my long string of mole traps for three days. By the fourth day, however, a thaw enabled me to walk off in the morning and gather my catch. I had not allowed for the bad walking conditions and the icy wind, and I was completely exhausted, with a blinding headache and numbed hands, long before I neared my home.

I was struggling along the Seven Tree Road, near Dead Man's Broom, when I looked across the intervening snow towards the 'new' road to Canada Farm and saw my brother Russell and a few others cycling on their way to Elveden Church to attend the funeral of the first Lady Iveagh, who had died on 16th February. I arrived home about two in the afternoon, and went straight to bed. That evening my father flayed the fourteen moles I had caught and tacked the skins out for me, though half of them were already spoiled by being left so long in the traps.

Dad realized that I should need a bicycle, and when an offer came along he bought one for ten shillings. The handlebars sloped downwards, with one handlegrip missing; it was very heavy and had a very high gear, but it was a means of getting about.

The next harvest time, David Wright asked me if I would help him to prepare the yealms for stack-thatching. A yealm is a tight, compact layer of wetted straw some fourteen to eighteen inches wide and four to six inches thick ready for the thatcher to lay on the stack. Both my father and Mr. Linney, the farm foreman, who wanted his stacks thatched, agreed I should take the job on, and after the first week I began to get the hang of it.

I had to stand sideways on and bend low to pull the straw from the bottom of the 'bed', the heap of long straw that had been wetted and left overnight to help straighten the straw. You drew from the bottom because the weight of the straw above would allow the wet straw to pull out straight.

As you pulled the stalks out you shuffled them forward in front of your legs, and laid them evenly. You worked from one end of the bed to the other, pulling out double handfuls of straw and laying them side by side. When you reached the end of the bed, the resulting quantity of straw was a yealm. Seven yealms were tied to a handle, what we called a yoke, and you then had a 'bunch' ready for carrying on to the stack for the thatcher to use.

After three days the tips of my fingers were raw and very painful. Hearing of my plight, a friend of mine came to Mr. Wright's house and brought a set of brass 'thimbles' for me to wear to protect my fingers. I'd wondered why he'd asked me to let him have my brass bicycle pump, now I knew!

After some of the stacks at Church Farm had been completed we were sent to thatch more at Canada Farm. It was a Monday morning, the wind almost at gale force, and I found that Canada Hill was too much for me to climb on my high-geared bicycle, so I was forced to dismount and walk. David, who was well ahead of me on his low-geared bike, stopped and waited, greeting me when I reached him with the words, 'What's it too much for you, met?'

I gained further thatching experience at Canada Farm, more at Avenue Farm, and finally we went back to Church Farm to finish off the remainder of the stacks there.

Just before I had started with the thatcher I had seen an advert in a daily newspaper for men's trousers which would 'Wear Like Wire'. That seemed just the thing for us, so I ordered two pairs, one each for Russell and myself. Within a week of starting to wear them my knees came through, and they were so rough they felt like wire.

Russell, who was loading on the waggons, found his also proved useless. That's no good making trousers out of wire!

In spite of my uncomfortable experiences I really enjoyed the thatching. When we had finished David Wright paid me far more than I should have received from the farm.

My first year on the farm I had to take a horse and tumbril along the 'back way' to a large heap of rough salt which had been carted there some time previously. I was met there by Squibby Macro, an Irish labourer who lived with his mother and sister. I had two shovels in the tumbril, and I was eager to show how willing I was to help, so I went straight to the big heap and tried to get a shovelful. To my surprise the salt was very hard.

Squibby, with Irish humour, said, 'Why, Edward, do you want to take the whole hape?' Then he showed me how to gradually scrape away the hard outer surface and reach the softer part further in. We loaded the tumbril, and then I had to drive the horse slowly up and down a field whilst Squibby spread the salt with his shovel.

My next job with Squibby was to lead the horse whilst he controlled the drill. We went to Telegraph Road and started on a field called 'Long Cranny'. The road end of the field was the lowest part, and it was uphill all the way. My horse, which was called Mack, had splayed feet. We went uphill and down with Squibby saying, 'Hold to you' or 'Hold off'. When we got to the top a second time Squibby looked back. 'No bloody eel could have squiggled down that wheel track,' he said.

One of my duties was to walk about a mile from my home to Mitchell's Farm, at the Bury St. Edmunds end of Icklingham village. In this farmyard were a number of heifers and a grizzly headed shorthorn bull that were turned out into an adjoining meadow each day. It was a simple matter to open the yard doors and let the animals wander out of the yard and through the meadow gateway, but when pasture became short on the first meadow it was necessary to drive the herd still further through into another meadow next to the River Lark.

I soon noticed that Tommy the bull appeared to resent my intrusion into the meadow, near the herd. He would skirt around the heifers, snort and scrape the ground with his forefeet, but eventually he would move off with the herd and I would shut the gate behind him. One evening I said to my father, 'I don't like the way that old bull behaves whilst I'm driving the animals across the meadow.'

'Why don't you take a good stick with you in case of trouble?' he told me, and promptly found for me a stout hazel netting stake.

Next morning I started out with more confidence. All went well until the cattle paused to graze on the brow of the slope in the first meadow, when Tommy detached himself from the group, trotted in a semi-circle towards the farmhouse wall which flanked the meadow, and began scraping the ground with his front hooves and snorting. I decided on an all-out attack, knowing that I was comparatively near a way of escape if necessary. With a flourish of the stick and a shout as I ran at the bull I succeeded in sending him back to the herd, still quietly grazing en route for the lower meadow.

The bull again adopted the same menacing attitude, tail out straight, nose to the ground, emitting a strange, short barking sound, and hooves scooping turf high over his back. Flushed with my first success I rushed at him again. Alas, this time he did not budge an inch! One last despairing glance convinced me that I was now too far from the fence to make a run for it. How often had I been warned, 'Never run away from a bull!'

I said aloud 'God help me!' and started to belabour the bull on its nose-ring. It backed a few paces as if preparing to charge and toss me, so I stepped forward and kept up the ceaseless blows with my stick, constantly repeating to myself, 'Dad says hit it right on the nose.'

After what seemed like an eternity, with the bull slowly retreating and I keeping my position close above its still lowered head, we came to the edge of a small disused pit. As the animal's hindquarters began to descend the sloping side, it became alarmed and with a final snort bounded sideways and ran downhill to rejoin the heifers, which had already reached the low meadow.

With a great sense of relief I also bounded down the hill to close the gate behind him. Going home to a belated breakfast, I felt as if I was walking on air.

The mood of triumph had somewhat dissipated by the next morning when I had to face up to the same prospect once again. My father had looked very grave at my news and suggested I take a pitchfork in case of further trouble. Duly armed with this weapon I opened the yard doors as usual, and out came the heifers to wend their way to the meadow. But where was the bull?

I soon discovered him standing quietly under the lean-to shelter in the yard. With some trepidation I approached, but he refused to move. It did not occur to me then that his nostrils must have been very sore from my treatment the previous day. After further efforts on my part he still would not move, and time was slipping away. Then I thought, why not try the fork? A slight touch might move him.

Again my lack of experience proved my undoing, for what I had estimated as a slight touch penetrated the bull's hide on the flank, and to my horror, strive as I might, I was powerless to withdraw the tine. At last the bull moved forward, pulling the fork from my grasp and taking it, still suspended from its flank, towards the middle of the yard.

Here he stopped, uncertain what to do with this troublesome thing. He decided to lean towards the fork, pushing the handle deep into the farmyard manure and driving the tines even further into himself. A final heave and the stout ash handle snapped like a matchstick, leaving part of the handle and the tines still attached to the bull, like a Red Indian's arrow in a buffalo.

I had watched all this petrified, but when the bull overturned the heavy wooden feed bin as if it were a matchbox, I leapt on to the farmyard doors as a place of safety, not knowing what the wounded animal might do next.

From my vantage point I saw a cowman, named Sid, coming home to his breakfast at the farmhouse. I hailed him, and together we went into the yard, where the bull had taken up his old position under the lean-to. With upraised stick I stood in front of the bull whilst my helper exerted all his strength and eventually extracted the fork.

At that moment I fancied I detected an expression of gratitude in the eyes of the bull. In the end we left him in the yard to regain his composure.

Not long after this incident I and another lad had to drive the bull some five miles along a public road to the village of Eriswell, where we thankfully left him at Chamberlain's Hall Farm.

Imagine my feelings when some months later I heard the news that a stockman had been tossed, trampled and seriously hurt by this same bull. The animal had to be driven off by another courageous stockman using a pitchfork! Later that day the bull was destroyed by a marksman using a rifle. In retrospect one wonders if the bull was taking revenge for the earlier incident with me.

Having turned out the stock at Mitchell's Farm before breakfast, I had to report for further orders to Church Farm each day after breakfast. One job I particularly disliked was weeding and sweeping up the farm entrance, which was flanked on one side by a low flint garden wall running down to the dairy. On the opposite side were horse and cattle yards.

One warm afternoon I was working steadily away when a man's voice interrupted me with a comment, 'Ted, you sweep just like an old woman!' I turned and saw that one of the horsemen had opened the chaff-house window, prior to feeding his team after a 'journey' at plough.

His sarcasm did not pass unnoticed. Presently he turned his back to me and leaned back on the window sill, head drooping forward as if he were dozing. I picked up one of the large clods of grass which I had been clearing away and slung it in the direction of my tormentor. The grass landed perfectly in the nape of his neck, loose soil falling down his open-necked shirt as he awoke with a start.

I prepared for a hasty flight, but all he said was, 'Ted, if you do that again, I'll hob your arse!'

Another lad about my age would also meet the foreman for orders. His favourite trick was to stand behind the foreman while the latter was speaking to me, making rude signs which only I could see. Sometimes the foreman would swing round unexpectedly, but he never caught him in the act.

We would be sent off to slash nettles and sheep's parsley wherever necessary, or to join two middle-aged women in heaping and burning twitch grass after it had been harrowed to the surface. I also had to feed poultry which had free range about three-quarters of a mile from the farm. With a pail of food on each arm I would set forth, only to have the foreman's young son follow me at what he thought was a safe distance, chanting, 'Bung, the little hen starver, coop, coop, coop!' I should explain that 'Teddy Bung' was my nickname at school (and, as I subsequently discovered, also the name of a well-known cartoon character).

Many times I tried to waylay him to exact vengeance, but he always succeeded in racing back to his mother just ahead of me, yelling as he went. In one way he had a point; the hens were half-starved, because the meal I was given to mix for them was of poor quality, whilst any so-called grain I ever had would blow away in the breeze, being mainly chaff. Bear in mind this was during the First World War, and food of any sort was scarce.

Another 'first time' job of mine ended disastrously. Stack-thatching had begun and I was told to go to a ditch with a large water cart, fill it and set it up ready for the thatcher next day.

I found the pump rusty and the washer dry, and pump away as I might the flow was painfully slow. Eventually, after much laborious work, the cart was filled and I went off to the appointed spot where the thatcher's 'bed' would be made. I decided to stand the cart with the shafts slightly up hill, to make emptying easier.

Having knocked up the back stick as tightly as I could, I let down the two set sticks on the shafts and gingerly unhooked the belly band. As soon as the horse moved forward the back stick slipped.

I held on to the shaft, but as my feet left the ground I decided to leave hold. Up went the shafts, pointing to the heavens, crash went the cart, and out went all the water. The thatchers were working about a half-mile away, and from the top of the stack had seen the incident. I rode the horse over to tell them what had happened.

They could see how crestfallen I was, and commented in a comforting tone 'There's plenty more water in the river!' They pumped and carted a load for themselves the following morning.

One Wednesday morning in May I had to rise quite early to meet a shepherd to help him drive a few of his flock to the market in Bury St. Edmunds. I had received my instructions overnight, and felt quite excited at the change of job for the day.

It meant a dusty eight-mile walk, or at times a run to get ahead to station myself in open gateways or side roads, whilst the shepherd brought up the rear. The cool, misty morn soon changed to blazing sunshine, and by the time we reached the town I was suffering from a severe headache.

Soon after we entered the streets of Bury, one of our charges, which doubtless felt the weight of its wool, bolted through the open doorway of a house, continued through the front room and finally settled under a table in the back kitchen. The back door leading into the garden was also open. I was trying to persuade the old ewe to leave when the startled lady of the house appeared at the back door. I had to apologise to her whilst the shepherd picked the sheep up bodily and deposited it back into the street. We rounded up the others and finally reached the market.

We repaired to a nearby tavern for bread and cheese, with beer for the shepherd and a mineral for me.

That same day I saw a beautiful shire mare named Janetta, from Church Farm, sold for seventy guineas, which seemed a very large sum of money to me at that time.

By the time we were thinking about the homeward journey I was feeling quite exhausted. On the Cornhill I met a shepherd from Elveden who knew my father; he noticed how poorly I looked and very kindly bought me a large juicy pear off one of the stalls.

I had just resigned myself to walking home and started off down St. Andrew's Street when along came an Eriswell lad driving a horse and tumbril at full trot. He offered me a lift, so I clambered in and off we went, cheered by the prospect of a ride home. A few yards down the road, out bounced the tailboard. I had to jump out and retrieve it, and had to hold it in the bottom of the vehicle thereafter because it had not been designed for jolting along the road at that pace. My headache had become almost unbearable by the time we reached Lackford, where we were overtaken by the Icklingham miller's son in a spring cart. Thankfully I changed over to the comparative comfort of the miller's cart to complete my homeward journey, and then went off to bed.

Next morning the foreman said, 'Where did you get to yesterday? I expected you back at work in the afternoon.'

On the farm 7

THE ensuing winter brought some very bitter weather, and deep snow. At this time I had to grind mangolds in the barn to mix with chaff, and then carry it in a large bag on my shoulders to a meadow where colts were turned out loose.

One particularly bad morning, with blizzard conditions, I went through the usual routine and struggled to the large feed bin standing in the meadow, with the colts running around me. The extra effort and the intense cold was too much for me, and suddenly I realised everything was turning black. If I fell there I might well be trampled by the hungry colts, so I managed to scramble into the bin for safety and laid down on the bag of food. After a time I came to with the colts snorting and milling all around the bin. I managed to empty the bag into the bin and make my way back to the farm.

On another occasion the foreman told me, 'Take a horse and tumbril, some rope and a fork and go to Mitchell's low meadow.' He and another man met me there, and soon my curiosity was satisfied. There, standing in a ditch up to its neck, was a young bullock, ice all round it, frozen to death.

With the aid of the fork and a good deal of patience a noose was fixed over its head, and the rope was tied to the tumbril. The horse pulled forward and the carcase was released and loaded into the vehicle. I was saddened to see this young creature die in such a manner; I had often counted the number in the meadow to check that they were all safe.

In due course I was given instruction in harnessing the heavy horses. Some of the gear appeared to weigh almost as much as I did at that time, but the 'old hands' were always ready to pass on helpful tips to overcome my lack of strength.

One Saturday morning I was told to take a horse and tumbril about two miles to another farm to bring back a load of mangolds from a 'reek'. Another farmworker, a few years my senior, was to come with a second vehicle. He had not been allowed to join up for military service because he was unduly affected by a full moon, and I had been warned not to upset him in any way. Therefore when he left his vehicle with the horse following me and wandered about picking up stones which he hurled in my direction, together with abuse, I just ignored him.

After half a mile of this he suddenly rejoined his conveyance and set off as fast as his horse could run, quickly passing me. I was glad of this temporary respite, but wondered what lay in store.

In due time I joined him at the 'reek' and began loading mangolds. He now bombarded me with these, especially the rotten ones which he

The Elveden Fire Brigade with their steam fire engine and wheeled fire escape in June, 1914. The driver, sitting slightly sideways on the driving seat of the engine, is William (Bill) Alderton, who was to be the author's father-in-law.

slung from his pitchfork, but I did not retaliate, and many of them helped to fill my tumbril. When his tumbril was about half full he suddenly drove off homewards. I stayed to complete my load, and it was some considerable time later that I saw my uneasy companion again. He was following behind his father, a small man, moving with a dejected hangdog air and shambling gait, arms hanging limply down. He took no further notice of me, for which I was very thankful.

My brother Ian lived most of his young life with my paternal grandmother at The Square, Eriswell. He worked at Chamberlain's Farm as a general farmhand and during this period was trained to hand milk. When our family moved to Elveden, Ian came with us and started work at High Lodge. He later became a gamekeeper on the Chalk Hall Beat and was a tremendous help to our father in the latter part of his life.

Ian was a kind, generous, gentle man, a devout Christian and supporter of the Church. He was married to Louisa Partridge, from Hockwold, and had one son, Edwin, who was tragically killed in a road accident in 1984, surviving his father by only three months.

Meanwhile, brother Arthur had been transferred from Icklingham to work as an apprentice carpenter at Elveden Clerk of the Works yard. He cycled to Elveden each Monday morning and returned on Saturdays at midday, lodging during the week at the Elveden Fire Station in a large room that was used as a dormitory for several unmarried employees.

In the evenings he would join Mr. A.G. Budden in his small cycle shop attached to the plumber's shop in the Clerk of the Works yard. As time went on Arthur would bring home all kinds of cycle equipment to sell on Mr. Budden's behalf, and he also did repair work on our own bicycles.

One evening he was fitting a new bicycle chain and asked me to hold a candle for him, our only means of lighting. He said to me, 'Hold it so you can see, then I can see.' I did so, and singed half the hair off his forehead! He had lovely hair which didn't look quite so good, and smelled awful, after that treatment!

With Arthur's tuition I became fairly useful, but lacked the necessary strength in my hands to do some of the cycle repairs.

One Sunday morning a knock came at our front door, Dad answered and I heard him say to the caller, 'My son is handy at that sort of thing.' He then brought in a soldier who had been on his way to Bury, but had got a flat tyre. Dad chatted to the man while I went through the normal tests, but I could find no puncture. I told him I could find nothing wrong, when to our amazement he said, 'Well I loosened the valve to let the air go in easier!' I tightened the valve, pumped up the tyre and he went on his way.

Whenever Arthur and I were working together he would always send me to the Post Office for a penn'orth of 'packers' for us to share; packers were small pieces of broken chocolate.

As time went on I was put in charge of a number of breeding sows at Roan Hall Farm, where some old stables and a horse yard had been adapted for this purpose.

When the litters arrived the problem of feeding became acute. Wartime restrictions on animal foods were so bad that the poor sows had to manage on something akin to thickened water, though the young ones were allowed a better quality meal. With the sows so ravenously hungry I had to devise a method of filling the outside troughs before releasing these madly screeching mothers into the yard, then quickly feeding the youngsters in their separate quarters before the sows returned and fiercely demanded to be admitted to grab any food the youngsters had not had time to eat.

I got the distinct impression that if I had not kept a sharp eye on them they would have eaten me as well, especially as I had a permanent layer of caked pig food adhering to the outside of my trouser legs where the pails rubbed. A few roots or cabbages when available also helped to keep them going.

Between pig-feeding times I had various jobs with horses. In previous years I had had experience of horse leading at harvest time and of riding the front binder horse, and I had found how useful a stout farm sack was in protecting one's rear from the sweat of the horse's back. I soon learned the importance of keeping straight ahead until the driver with the self-binder was ready to turn, then bearing sharp left ready to resume the pulling again. Another thing that was impressed on me was the vital importance of shouting 'hold ye' before starting the waggon.

Each of those great shire horses was an individual. Old Bella, so calm and steady; Edie with the high withers, uncomfortable to ride bareback; Frank with the stiff knees, who when walking appeared to move like a wooden horse, although he was adept at keeping the tees just tight without undue exertion.

One very hot morning my brother Russell and I had Bella in a scotch cart, loading up an old stack bottom to be carted away for litter. We had about half a load when the old mare fell down flat in the shafts and appeared to be dead. Whilst we were considering what to do next the animal struggled to its feet and supported the cart again. We thereupon set the cart up on its set sticks and led the mare to a shady stable. When we informed the foreman at lunchtime he examined the mare and came to the conclusion that she had simply fallen down fast asleep! After all, she was twenty years old.

One hot August afternoon I was sent off to cart some 'rakings' from a field which had been cleared of sheaves. With Frank between the shafts of the tumbril I had nearly completed my task when a sudden thunderstorm brought torrential rain sweeping across the open field. I was in my shirt-sleeves and decided the best shelter I could get was to crouch underneath the tumbril. Shelter there certainly was, but only a foolish boy would have taken the risk. One startled movement by Frank and I could have been run over by either wheel or been trampled underfoot. In the event, as the fury of the storm raged all about us, Frank stood with his head down, steady as a rock.

Then there was Iona, a nervous mare, a willing worker, and an armchair ride. I was leading this mare through the village with a high waggon load of straw and we had reached a narrow point with a high bank on one side and two cottage doorsteps jutting out on the other. Over the brow of the hill came an army motor lorry, the first I had ever seen, with canvas hood billowing in the wind. Iona stopped, stared with head held high, and as the noisy lorry drew near she gave a little jump and I had to hold on tight. Next moment the frightening thing had passed and the startled mare regained control of the loaded waggon, which had just begun to pull her back down the slope.

Isabel, an exceptionally strong mare, would work her heart out. I have seen her swoon and fall in her traces after tugging at a heavy load, with Frank not doing his share in the shafts.

I remember when Isabel had had her first foal, and the time came for her to gradually get back to work. Therefore, quite early one morning, Frank Childerstone, the horsekeeper, took Isabel in his team for ploughing. About two hours later I was told to go with a relief horse and bring Isabel back to her foal. The exchange was duly made and the horseman said to me, 'Do you want to ride back?' He fixed the plough trace to act as stirrups, then gave me a leg up.

We had started from the far end of a long field. Presently the mare began to trot, then broke into a comfortable gallop. We were nearing the bottom of the field when I realized that we had to round the end of an elm row and turn at right angles into a cart track with high quarters. My experience of riding was nil. I tried to steady the mare, but with the thought of her foal uppermost in her mind she took no notice of my puny efforts, just slackened enough to round the corner, with me clinging like a leech to her long mane to keep my seat, which I did with great difficulty.

There was no stopping her now, gallop she would all the way home. As she thundered into the farmyard the waiting foreman stood aghast. 'I told you to walk,' he yelled at me. 'Now I shall have to wait for half an hour for her milk to cool before I put her to the foal.'

I did point out that my intentions had been good, but that the mare had brought me and I had little choice in the matter. Never shall I forget that ride!

Kitty was the only jibber on the farm, and vicious with it. One look at her ears laid back, whites of eyes showing, and twitching 'rat' tail was sufficient warning to look out for trouble. Once safely between the shafts of a tumbril, the instruction to go forward invariably brought a very sudden reverse, accompanied by a splaying front foot and bared teeth.

One morning the foreman sent me off on Kitty's back to do some rolling. This comfortable ride was the only thing I enjoyed about that morning's work. Arriving at the field, I succeeded in fixing the mare up ready for the word 'go'. Knowing the animal's reputation, I stood beside the roll with my long driving cords and said 'gee up'. This was the signal for Kitty to come backwards at a great rate. I have often wondered how far back she might have gone, but this field was flanked by a belt of sturdy Scots fir trees; bang went the frame of the roll square against the trees, with Kitty striving against her breechings to push them down.

I hit her flank with a long hazel stick which I had found on the roll, and she leapt forward at full speed, with me holding on to the cords attempting to keep her on a straight course. I did not succeed, and on my return across the field I had to go over my zig-zag tracks to make them look presentable. My next start was a repetition of the first, with more zig-zag work to iron out, but gradually the mare settled and I made better progress. Nevertheless, when the foreman visited me later he remarked in his Lincolnshire accent, 'Oi, yew 'aven't doon mooch!'

Mick had been badly broken, with the result that his mouth was 'hard' on the near side. One afternoon I set off on Mick's back to visit the blacksmith, about a mile along the village street in the opposite direction to Mick's favourite meadow. He ignored my tugs to keep him in the right direction and headed for his meadow. I thereupon brought him round in a circle and tried again with the same result. After a third attempt someone spotted my dilemma and led Mick a little further up the street and he gave me no more trouble.

Mack was a loose, ambling horse with splayed front hooves, and it was difficult for a boy to lead him without some risk of having his foot trodden on. One cold, frosty morning I was 'driving away' muck tumbrils, that is, accompanying the full load from yard to field and returning with the empty vehicle. My route was along a green road culminating in a sharp turn over a bank, through a gap in the hedge and on to the field. Whilst negotiating this awkward place I suddenly felt Mack's hoof descending on my foot. I screamed as I anticipated crushed bones and crippling pain; nothing happened. The horse had instantaneously shifted his weight, knowing that it was my foot he was touching, aided by the fact that my boots were covered with icy rime frost and very slippery.

There was another mare which I have not yet mentioned, her name was Polly. She had been transferred from the Game Department, where she had been used for carting rabbits in a light spring cart or for journeys by road. Polly had sustained a nasty fetlock injury which necessitated her being confined to a loose box for three weeks. At the end of this time the foreman said to me, 'Take Polly with some bags of food for the colts in the meadow near Snakes Island.' I was a bit dubious about this assignment, but duly obeyed.

My route lay through two meadows and into a third. Polly behaved perfectly whilst I opened the third gate and led her over a very narrow bridge, closing the gate behind me. I had to make a detour in this meadow to get round the end of a ditch which extended half way across; the other side was bounded by the River Lark. Soon I reached the feed trough and proceeded to empty the bags of food. But where were the colts?

I had just taken up my position in the empty cart ready to return when suddenly, from behind the shelter of the trees on Snakes Island, came a bunch of colts galloping towards the trough. This was too much for Polly, who could hear but not see them because of her blinkers.

She panicked, and off she went at full speed. I felt like Ben Hur as I hung on to one rein to keep her from veering into the aforementioned ditch. I succeeded in keeping her out of the ditch, and as we rounded the end she pelted towards the narrow bridge, stopping on this with her chest pressing at the gate.

With the prospect of plunging into the river at any moment I had no alternative but to climb out of the cart and open the gate. This I did, but before I could regain control she bolted madly off, knocking down a gatepost as she passed. When I arrived back at the farm on foot someone had taken charge of the mare. As I was unhurt, little was said except by a young friend of mine who had witnessed the incident. His comment was, 'I didn't dare look, I thought you'd been killed!'

In the summer months the horses would be turned into the meadows after they had been fed and brushed following the day's work. The horseman would allow the lads to ride these horses down to the chosen meadow. I usually rode the aforementioned Isabel. Sometimes a race would develop and we would dismount at the greatest distance possible from the stable. One day we heard one of our number yelling for help. Looking back we saw he had fallen under the neck of his mount and was clinging on there with arms and legs, not daring to drop his feet to the ground for fear of being run over.

At another period of my time at Church Farm there was a small heifer turned out to graze in a meadow next to the River Lark. I can recall seeing this crazy young thing bellowing across the river to a bull which was running with older heifers in another meadow. The water was unusually low at the time. Finally the heifer crossed the river to the bull, with the inevitable result.

Eventually the time came when she was due to calve. She had been put into a small place and tied to a ring attached to a manger. There she had unfortunately caught one horn in this ring and wrenched off all the hard outer covering, leaving the inner part bare and bleeding. At this point her calving began. Cowman Sid went in response to her cries of pain and had a difficult task ahead, so with no-one else available he called on me to help.

This was the first and only calving I have ever witnessed. This small, sad creature had an extremely difficult and painful time; in the midst of it all Sid said, 'Serve you right, you shouldn't have swum across the river to the bull!'

This heifer must have been a born loser. She remained undersized and was disfigured by the loss of one horn, so a decision was taken to send her to market. My brother Russell was also on the farm at this time, restarting after a bout of ill health, and it fell to him to drive this unfortunate animal to Bury market. He made uneventful progress as far as Flempton, but there his charge slipped through a gap in the hedge and led him a merry chase over the golf course. Time after time he headed her off as she instinctively bolted for home, but finally he became exhausted and as she outran him he despairingly hurled his stick in her direction.

To his amazement the heavy knob caught her bang on the side of her nose. She swung completely round, and with renewed hope Russell managed to get her back on to the road and then continued on his eight-mile journey to a successful conclusion.

At the market tavern Russell met a few acquaintances from Eriswell and a drink or two followed. He also arranged to have a lift home in a cattle float drawn by two horses and driven by a diminutive horsekeeper from Eriswell named Harry Leonard. When they started for home, Harry was already in a happy mood, perched high on the driving seat. This elevated position gave him an excellent view of the countryside, and when nearing Fornham All Saints he pulled his horses to a halt in order to shout some biting criticism to two farmworkers who were drilling on an adjacent field. The men merely waved and laughed at his comments. Another stop was made at Fornham Three Kings, where Harry stalked in with a call for a quart, insisting that Russell helped to drink it, in spite of the fact that he had already had too much!

Then on at a lumbering trot to Icklingham, where Harry found it impossible to pass The Plough Inn. Once again the cry was for a quart and insistence that Russell must share it. As the inn door swung to behind Harry, so Russell was able to escape. He made his way home by means of the roadside fence to steady his uncertain steps, in no state to touch another drop.

Memories of war, 1914-18 8

ONE sunny Saturday morning I was reading a book, sitting on the garden wall overlooking the street and facing towards the River Lark, some quarter of a mile away, when suddenly I heard the sound of an aircraft engine.

Looking up, I saw an aeroplane flying just above the river, obviously using it as a guide from Bury St. Edmunds to Mildenhall, where the 1912 Army manoeuvres were taking place. Large numbers of ground troops were employed in this exercise.

I had heard on the 'grapevine' that Colonel Cody was engaged as a spotter pilot to assist the army, so this must have been him. Little did I know then that the War Office had chosen Cody's aircraft as the preferred model over thirty-two others submitted. It was designated Army Aeroplane Number One.[1]

Somewhat later we heard one Saturday evening that an aeroplane had landed in a small meadow in Mildenhall. The next morning was cold and windy, but in spite of the weather we decided to go and have a look. Russell had a bicycle on which he offered me a lift. This meant placing my left foot on the 'step' fixed to the rear wheel spindle, with my right knee resting on the carrier at the back! Thus we travelled to Mildenhall and found the plane.

Apparently the pilot, Donald Parker, had flown from the Royal Flying Corps base at Snare Hill in Norfolk to spend the night with his parents, members of the Parker family who owned the well-known and respected milling firm, Parker Bros. Soon after we had joined other spectators at the scene, Donald and his family appeared and we were asked to hold on to the frame of the plane by the wires while the engine was started by swinging the propeller.

[1] In fact more than a score of aeroplanes and an airship flew no fewer than 7,855 miles during the 1912 manoeuvres.

There was a mighty roar and a rushing wind as the engine fired, and we hung on as the engine warmed up. I began to wonder if the plane was going to tilt over, but we were told to jump away and the plane sped off, just clearing the trees on the opposite side of the meadow.

At the outbreak of the 1914-18 War, an Ammunition Column was stationed at Icklingham, while the guns were stationed at Tuddenham, four or five miles away the other side of the Lark. Six of the men were billeted in our front room. Often the column would parade and then assemble, with their officers, and meet the guns at a given point before commencing a route march.

We boys were very interested in all this and soon got to know many of the soldiers when they were off duty. Two of the officers, from a well-to-do local county family, were billeted at Icklingham Hall.

Some beautiful horses were stabled in our thatched barn, which had been requisitioned by the army. The big barn doors were closed at night, and two pickets were posted outside to keep guard over the horses which were ranged along the inside of the barn wall. A small doorway had been cut through the back wall of the barn and gave much-needed ventilation. When we were indoors we could plainly hear the horses moving about.

The horses were fed and groomed early in the morning, then at about ten o'clock the two officers from The Hall would walk into the yard, looking very smart in their uniforms. There would be a very careful inspection. The whole procedure was of great interest to me as I watched through our back window.

About eight each evening my mother would make a large jug of hot cocoa for me to take over to the pickets on duty. The men were very grateful for this. Mum would often say to me, 'They are somebody's boys!'

A week or two later I was sitting on our meadow gate when I noticed a small group of soldiers gathered outside the small doorway at the back of the barn. A sergeant was in charge and he ordered the men to form a ring. Then I noticed a tall thin private had boxing gloves on; his opponent, whom I recognized as Trumpeter Whyard, a much smaller man, was also wearing gloves. The N.C.O. gave the order to start, and after the first round it was obvious to me that the trumpeter was much the better boxer of the two. His opponent kept striking out, but his blows were parried and return punches went in like lightning! The uneven contest was over in three rounds, whereupon they shook hands.

About a fortnight after this affair, something occurred which has stayed in my mind all my life. Once again I was sitting on the gate at the bottom of the meadow. I noticed a few soldiers had gathered outside the barn; one man was given a send off as he mounted a powerful horse and rode out into the meadow. My mother's linen line was situated about half way across the meadow, near to a six-foot-wide path. He sped across the meadow to the path and up to the top gate, then turned and with extra speed thundered down the middle.

Obviously he was unaware of the linen line until the last moment. The horse's head just went under the wire, the rider made a desperate attempt to ward off the line with one hand, but the line caught him on his neck and dragged him off. He swung back on the line, then slipped off into a crumpled heap on the ground. His companions, like me, had watched this in horror and rushed to his aid. I watched miserably as he was carried away unconscious.

I did not hear any more of him for three days, then one morning I was going to the Post Office when I saw the soldier coming towards me on foot. He had left his neck, throat and chest bare, and I could see they were black and blue. I was glad to see he was still alive and able to walk about.

In our house, standing so close to all the activity, we could hear many unusual noises both night and day. There would be troops moving from a canteen at The Maltings, which had been requisitioned, or from another canteen situated in the large barn at Church Farm, where I used to grind mangolds.

One moonlit night as I lay in my little bedroom I could hear a loud wailing sound, like someone in acute pain. It continued for hours, and my poor mother was much distressed. I knew that one form of army punishment was to strap an offender's arms and legs in a cruciform position to a wagon wheel. This somewhat barbaric punishment, called 'First Field Punishment', soon caused numbness and cramp; it was only used for serious offences. Mother and I listened half the night, and once again she said sadly, 'He is some mother's boy.' Next day we learned that a soldier had indeed been punished by this method on the wheel of an ammunition wagon positioned in a nearby field, once the Cricket Meadow.

Soon after war broke out Dad had instructions to send rabbits and any other items like pigeons or wild duck to Elveden. A dealer from Brandon had obtained the trade instead of Mr. How from Freckenham.

As soon as the warreners brought the rabbits in, we loaded them in the cart and Bob Levett, the driver, set off for Elveden Game Larder, some five miles away. We knew the approximate time when Bob should return home, but on one particular occasion he was over an hour late. At long last we heard him pull into the yard. Dad went out to help him stable the horse, then brought Bob to the back door and said, 'Come and sit down.' I then noticed Bob had taken off his cap and was holding his head which had a nasty cut in it. He said, 'I'm wounded!'

After Dad had attended to the injury and Bob had gone home, Dad told me what had happened. After Bob had left Elveden he turned off the main road, taking the Seven Tree Road as a short cut to Icklingham. All went well until he was opposite Dead Man's Broom, when a covey of English partridges flew up under the horse's head, causing the horse to rear. Bob and the seat were shot out of the back of the cart, and he cut his head in the process. Fortunately the frightened animal made no attempt to bolt, and by talking gently to him Bob was able to calm him down.

In due course Mr. Linney, the farm bailiff, received a message from the War Office informing him that their eldest son, William Francis Linney (he had the same names as his father), had been seriously wounded and was in hospital. Mrs. Linney immediately rushed off on her bicycle to catch a train from Mildenhall Station, with her mind so set on the reason for her journey that she failed to brake at the difficult corner in Barton Mills and ran into a fence. Her hands and knees were so badly hurt that Mr. Linney had to go and fetch her in his horse and cart.

A fortnight later, Mrs. Linney had recovered and when I went to Church Farm for orders I was told to drive her to Mildenhall Station so that she could make the journey to see her son, who, I am pleased to say, recovered.

In due time all the beautiful horses stabled in our barn were transferred elsewhere. They were replaced by some Mexican mules, which must have been some the Mexicans wanted to be rid of! Those animals knew every awkward trick under the sun!

The pickets on guard at night had constant trouble from their kicking, biting, breaking loose and making noises that only mules can emit. We were often awakened by them. Periodically they had to be clipped according to army regulations. One particular sergeant seemed to be the expert, with no fear of mishap.

I had previously watched him clipping the horses, which was a fairly simple business. Usually they would strap up one foreleg, then one man would stand at the horse's head while another would do the clipping. These mules were a very different story, needing more men to control them. An unsuccessful start was made with one of the animal's forelegs strapped up; soon a second leg was secured after much difficulty.

One mule, I recall, had to be thrown down and had three of its legs tied with cords. The struggling beast managed to loosen its bonds, somehow became upright and staggered, still partially bound, to the closed meadow gate. It placed its one free leg on top of the gate and hopped right over! The clipping was abandoned for that day. I think the men were more exhausted than the mule!

Next day the team started by 'throwing' the mule and securing all four legs! They did some clipping, but only with great difficulty.

When the Ammunition Column moved on it was replaced by the Royal Defence Corps, and again six of the men were billeted with us. Their uniforms were a dark greyish blue, a distinct contrast to the khaki we had become used to with our previous lodgers.

This unit, composed largely of men too old for military service, with a stiffening of regular soldiers, had been drafted into the area to guard the perimeter of a large section of heathland around Canada Farm and Bernersfields. This area, stretching for many miles between Elveden and Icklingham, became a top secret testing and training ground for the first tanks, which later went into action on the Western Front[2]. A double ring of soldiers was deployed around this area, with the older men forming the outer ring and the regular soldiers the inner.

Dad had long suspected that something most unusual was going on from the terrible noises he heard; he said it sounded like 'the engines of Hell!' All were sworn to secrecy. My brother Arthur subsequently joined the Tank Corps, serving on the Western Front until he was wounded.

I soon resumed my 9 p.m. habit of taking a jug of cocoa in to them, which was much appreciated. When my dad had time to talk to the soldiers he found that they were to guard the section from Canada Farm to Gibson's Lodge, the line of the private road from the main road, now the A11, to Icklingham.

One of the men billeted with us was a clock and watchmaker whose wife was trying to keep the business going during his absence. He was allowed more off-duty time in order to catch up with his work. They were a very friendly set of men, and when their duties came to

[2] The first tanks were built by William Foster & Co. Ltd. of Lincoln in 1915. The name 'tank' was a cover, adopted after it had been suggested they be referred to as 'water carriers' and some wit in the works had referred to 'That bloody tank!' The original term 'landship' had been a give-away. As they came off the production line the new tanks were delivered to the training camp at Elveden, where the first mock battle, witnessed by Lloyd George, took place on 16th June, 1916. For an account of the early development of the tank see Michael R. Lane, *The Story of the Wellington Foundry, Lincoln, A History of William Foster & Co. Ltd.*, Unicorn Press, 1997.

Men of the Royal Defence Corps outside the Turner home at Icklingham with the author's two sisters. Six of these men were billeted there.

an end they presented my mother with a lovely clock as a parting gift. At the end of February, 1916, the Elveden Estate Game Department was completely disbanded and the younger men were expected to join up in the armed forces. Arthur had joined the 'Heavy Section' of the Machine Gun Corps, which was the undercover name given to what later became the Tank Corps. He was initially stationed near Grantham in Lincolnshire and later at Bovington, Dorset.

The older men were absorbed into other departments, chiefly 'Farms' and 'Woods'. My father and a warrener named Joe Bailey chose the latter, but were always available for farm work during haysel and harvest.

There was a great deal of work to do on the farm, but because of the number of men who had joined the Forces there were fewer to do the work. The low meadows had to be cut for hay, then there was the hot job of turning it and putting it into rows and finally the carting, when care had to be taken to avoid the swampy places.

One memorable day every vehicle and every horse possible were mustered to clear the meadows near Temple Bridge. Sometimes three horses were necessary to get a loaded wagon off the meadow on to the firm cart track leading back to the village. It was late evening before all the loaded waggons and carts had been brought off the meadows. They rumbled their way through the village to the farm, a brilliant full moon overhead, and were lined up in the stackyard ready for unloading in the morning. The horses were fed and the men went wearily home to their war rations and bed.

Often, as members of the St. John Ambulance Brigade, these same men would be called to unload Red Cross ambulance trains full of wounded soldiers at Ingham or Bury St. Edmunds, working until the early hours, but they always turned up for work in the morning at the appointed time. These men had received considerable training for a long period before the war, and proved their worth when hostilities broke out.

A telegram would be sent to my father advising the time of arrival at Icklingham of an ambulance to convey the volunteer ambulancemen to the station at which the train was expected. He had to pass on this message to the individuals concerned, who lived in a scattered community with three outlying farms, Avenue, Canada and Bernersfields. Fortunately the members of his family were mobile, and we were dispatched to all points of the compass. Many a dark and stormy night have we young messengers, my sister May included, traversed the rough and lonely tracks to deliver the vital message while my father changed into his St. John Ambulance uniform.

He told me many of these wounded men, often caked with mud from the battlefield, looked as if they had come straight from hell, which indeed they had. He dreaded that the time might come when he would see my eldest brother Arthur amongst the injured. As it turned out, when Arthur was wounded he was sent to a hospital in Cheltenham.

Wartime farming 9

IN MARCH, 1916, there was a terrible blizzard, bringing heavy snow. Bitter winds flattened hundreds of trees, huge gaps were torn in the old Scots fir belts intersecting the fields, and some huge black poplars which marked the line of the River Lark were blown down. One of these fell athwart the stream, forming a complete dam, about midway between the Three Bridges and the water mill. Soon the waters had topped the south bank and the meadows were flooded. At this stage my father and Joe were called to clear the obstacle.

A stout flat-bottomed boat was obtained from the miller, Mr. Carl Marston. Then, furnished with axes and an exceptionally long crosscut saw, they set to work, sometimes with one man in the boat and the other standing on the huge trunk. By concentrating on the upper sections of the tree a channel was cleared to let the water flow. Gradually the great limbs were severed and floated to the bank. Finally the enormous trunk was cut into sections that were hauled ashore by an Estate steam engine, and left lying in the Dispensary Meadow to disintegrate with the passing of the years.

For much of that summer my father and Joe were kept busy cutting up the blown-down trees for firewood, which was badly needed by all and sundry.

As harvest time approached they joined the 'gang' required to cart and stack the corn which was being cut by the horse-drawn self-binders. I was with the party as a horse leader. One hot and dusty day a large stone bottle of beer was sent for and solemnly dispensed in the traditional manner: One man agreed to be 'pourer', and his right was to drink both first and last. Balancing the stoneware bottle on his knee, he would fill the 'tot', exercise his right, then refill it and hand it round to the circle of men until all had received their share. I declined to have any beer, but watched the proceedings with interest, especially when the man who emptied the last tot said, 'That's poor lap!', a reflection on the poor quality of beer prevailing at that period of the war.

Quite soon after that episode everyone began to have hot tea brought out to them by their relatives to drink with their 'fourses' instead of beer!

With the advent of the self-binder for cutting the corn the old rules which my father had told me about the use of scythes no longer applied, but I repeat them here as a matter of interest.

The 'lord' of the harvest would be appointed by the farmer. He must needs be a good man at harvest work in general, taking the lead in all the operations, and constituting a trustworthy link between master and men. Any young men who had not previously taken a harvest would be called 'colts', and would be expected to pay for a gallon of beer.

Great pride was taken in the way the work was done, the best men setting a high standard for the less skilled to attain if they could. On the first day rules would be made about various procedures, and thereafter they were strictly enforced. For instance, the fine for each offence of swearing at meal-times would be a penny, and if not paid would be stopped at the end of the week. The revenue from such fines would invariably be spent on beer.

The youngest 'colt' would be called the 'lady', and he would follow next to the 'lord' when mowing. The 'lady' would also be the book-keeper for the fines, provided he could read and write.

After being mown, the corn lay in neat swathes which would then be pushed together by the men with their feet, or a 'toppler' might be used. Each man then proceeded to tie the corn into sheaves, making his tie bands from straw. The sheaves were then 'shocked' or 'stooked' in the usual manner, and the land carefully raked afterwards.

In 1915 there was still a 'lord' who 'took' the harvest on behalf of a number of men, agreeing a fixed sum to get the harvest in. The farm foreman usually consulted him whenever it was necessary to make decisions such as when to cut or when to cart.

Old farmers would note especially that the barley was well 'bridled' before cutting. Barley and oats must be very dry before carting, whereas wheat, if ripe, would often be carted even when damp. Barley was always carted loose, after being run together with large three-tined shack forks.

When all the cornfields had been cut the task of carting and stacking began. In my second year I was entrusted with 'driving away', which entailed taking charge of a loaded waggon and walking with the horses to the nearest stackyard. Then one had to come back to the same harvest field with the empty waggon to be reloaded. Sometimes a trace-horse was dispensed with for 'driving away' and was left on the field to be used where it was most needed.

With the harvest work well advanced, I was sent up the Telegraph Road to a field which had been harvested that year after laying fallow for many years. I took an old-fashioned horserake and a steady horse. I soon realized the rake was going in too deep, making the poor horse go into a lather. I tried to alter the rake, but it was so rusty that I could not adjust it. By this time my rakings were full of sand.

About mid-morning Mr. Linney, the foreman, visited me. He tried to adjust the rake, but to no avail, so he decided we must leave what few rakings there were on the field.

For my next job I was sent with three other men to clear some rakings from another field. We had a waggon and two horses; two of the men were loading, and the other man and I were on the load. The rakings amounted to three-quarters of a load. Having cleared the field, we took a short cut through the trees surrounding the field. Suddenly I felt the load was about to slide sideways; the man with me saw the look of alarm on my face. I said to him, 'What would you do if the load slid sideways?' His answer was 'Run like hell the other way!' Fortunately the load remained where it was.

Russell was given a retriever dog to take care of by one of the soldiers. With the food shortage at that time Russell and I decided to go down towards Temple Bridge with the dog to see if we could find some rabbits. We stopped under the alder trees that lined the river bank, whereupon, the dog, Joffre, named after the Commander-in-Chief of the French army at the time, started jumping up and searching for rabbits in the reeds. He made several lightning kills, but it was a warm evening and as he was panting so much, we were concerned for his welfare.

However, we could not stop him until he had killed all the rabbits he could find. Russell and I counted them and there were forty! Full of admiration for what Joffre had accomplished, we gutted them at once, so that they were lighter to carry home.

One cold morning when the wind seemed to be near gale force I went to Church Farm at 6 a.m. as usual. Suddenly a tall man dressed in overalls appeared, obviously in a distressed state of mind.

'Can you tell me where I can find a policeman?' he blurted out. I said, 'Yes, just round the corner.'

'My mate has just had his coat blown into the pulley belt of the tractor and it has killed him!' the man told me as he went off to P.c. Sladden's house.

I decided to jump on my bike and go up to Mitchell's Farm to report the tragic news. There I found my father, who was amongst the men unloading a waggon. Mr. Linney, the foreman, was also there, and it was decided that a party of men should go to Bernersfields at once to give whatever help was needed. I heard later that the man who had brought the news to me was Victor Dann of Thetford.

Not many weeks had elapsed before I was told to report to Mr. James Ashen, Lord Iveagh's chauffeur from Elveden, at Brand Pin Field, where an Overtime tractor, an oil-engined tractor imported from America, was hauling a plough. Mr. Ashen said, 'Boy, would you like to drive a tractor?' I told him that I was willing to be taught, but that I had had no previous experience.

To my surprise he told me to climb into the driver's seat, and he then showed me the various controls and what they were used for. I tried to remember everything, but found it difficult to hear what was said because of the loud noise of the tractor engine.

'We might as well make a start,' Mr. Ashen told me after he had given me my instructions. He stood beside me with his hand gripping a handle which he himself had fitted in the large wheel guard and shouted 'Let the clutch in *gently*.'

I immediately lifted my foot off the pedal, and the tractor leapt forward. Out of the corner of my eye I saw Jim Ashen disappear, and then rapidly reappear as he hauled himself back up one-handed and yelled, 'I said GENTLY!'

'Sorry, I didn't hear your last word,' I said. His thoughtful provision of the hand grip had undoubtedly saved his life, otherwise he would have been under the spiked iron wheel of the plough!

I had a good long session learning the method of turning at the end and setting into the right furrow to return down the field. I realized I was needed to drive up and down whilst Mr. Ashen had a break.

Later Arthur Bailey, another chauffeur from Elveden, joined us. I noticed they spent a lot of time looking for plovers' eggs in what I knew was a favourite spot. They did vouchsafe to me that Lord Iveagh had sent them a message to try and find some for him.

One day, just after dinner, I had to go to Church Farm to collect a letter which James had written to Mr. William Levick at the Elveden Estate Office about something he needed for the tractor. As usual I was told to hurry. Having cycled to Elveden, I saw Mr. William Levick, who sent me to The Stables to find his brother, Mr. Fred Levick, who would be working there at his lathe.

I left the Estate Office and biked into the Game Yard entrance and then along to the Stables, through the archway and across the yard to the workshop. Mr. Levick's brother read the letter, then hunted around to find the part needed. Meanwhile I stood somewhat overawed by the height and size of the building, so much larger than anything I had ever seen at Icklingham.

When I got back with the spare part James was able to carry out the repair.

The Brand Pin Field was eventually finished, and the next destination was a field next to the Telegraph Road. The outfit was prepared for road travel by having covers placed over the spiked wheels and the caravan, normally used by the steam roller, was taken in tow.

Things were very difficult in wartime, with serious shortages of food, and as time went on it became obvious that Mother was not at all well. She had contracted tuberculosis, an illness that in those days was largely incurable. After the worry of Dad's illness and with the constant strain of caring for a large family, she was in no state to fight the debilitating illness.

Before long it became obvious that Mother was weakening, and soon she was confined to her bedroom. We children were only allowed to say ‘Goodnight, Mum’ through the open door as we went to bed. Dad realized he must have help in the house to care for Mother, someone to prepare a hot dinner for us when we came out of school and also a meal for himself at mid-day.

Dad called on Mr. and Mrs. David Wright to ask if Mrs. Wright could spare the time to do this work. They themselves had a family of four daughters, but after talking it over Mrs. Wright agreed to come.

Mother's condition was such that it was necessary for Russell to make an evening trip to the Mildenhall surgery for further medication. That same evening we heard an air raid warning, followed soon afterwards by the sound of engines. Running outside, we clearly saw the cigar-shaped Zeppelin gleaming in the moonlit sky. At the same time a heavy naval gun was being towed through the village, to be set up at the Barton Mills crossroads, where it was fired repeatedly at the Zeppelin without success. Later still the gun returned to its base in Bury St. Edmunds.

Russell and his friend returned from Mildenhall, somewhat shaken, to report that they had just arrived at Barton Mills when the naval gun opened up. They had thrown themselves in fright into an roadside ditch, narrowly avoiding a ducking in the water at the bottom.

The next day we heard that the Zeppelin had dropped bombs on a field in the Rows at Eriswell, mistaking twitch grass fires for an army camp (it was customary to burn the clumps of dug-up twitch grass in order to destroy it).

Mother's condition worsened, and soon Dad had to have a special open-air hut belonging to the Estate erected in our garden under the large apple tree. Fresh air was about the only cure known for TB in those days. In the hut there was room for a large bed so that my parents could spend all night in the open, then return to the house in the morning.

In March, 1917, Doctor Glazier told Dad to send for the nearest relatives if they wished to see mother alive. An urgent message was relayed to Arthur's commanding officer, bringing a reply that we must get confirmation of mother's illness from our village Rector before Arthur could be released. Dad hurried to the vicarage to obtain the necessary confirmation, which was sent off immediately.

Train services were already overtaxed, due to war conditions, and Arthur found that the only station he could get to was Higham, near Bury St. Edmunds. He arrived there in the early hours and walked the eight miles home, where I was keeping a look out for him.

He came in and said, 'Hello, mate,' to me and was then greeted by Mrs. Linney, who had come in to help us. She threw her arms around him and they both burst into tears. After a few minutes, during which Arthur regained his composure, Mrs. Linney said, 'You are too late, your mother died a few minutes ago.'

Arthur made his way upstairs to join our father who was sitting beside Mother's bed. I went through our meadow gate to the kennel, where Dad's favourite bitch, Dora, was kept. In tears I said to the dog, 'My mother is dead,' and put my arms around her. She knew I was upset, and smothered my face and hands with affectionate licks.

A few days later we all attended Mother's funeral, which seemed to be attended by everyone in the village. The burial spot was near the yew bush, close to the churchyard wall; my friend Colin Linney's headstone was nearby. For many years after we had moved to Elveden Alan Linney looked after Mother's grave for us.

Arthur had his leave extended until after the funeral. I was so proud of him, because he was the only soldier in Icklingham wearing the Tank Corps uniform.

Elveden game larder 10

IN JANUARY, 1919, the family moved to Elveden when my father took up residence in the Head Gamekeeper's Lodge. He had become Head Gamekeeper in 1916, but with the war being on had remained at Icklingham. He took over from Mr. Allen Hill, who himself had succeeded his father, Mr. William Hill.

My brother Russell was at this time an apprentice at Chiver's Farm learning about poultry keeping, and Ian was working as a general farmhand at High Lodge; he later followed in Dad's footsteps and became a gamekeeper.

My job was to be in the game larder and game office. I remember meeting Charlie Linge, who was then in charge of the game larder, for the first time when he walked into the game office and I said, 'Good morning, Mr. Linge.' 'My bloody name is Charlie!' he said, and so it stayed from then on.

Part of my job was to do the weekly wage packets for the gamekeepers, warreners, and wire fence men, to write up the Warreners' Book and the Game Registers, and to sell rabbits and pheasants, etc., from the game larder. I also had to write up the game cards for each gun for the day's shoot; they had to be delivered to the Hall each evening in time for the butler to hand them to Lord Iveagh at dinner.

When Dad had planned each shoot I had to type several copies to distribute to Lord Iveagh, his private secretary, Mr. C.H. Bland, the Estate Office and the gamekeepers at Eriswell and Icklingham. After each shoot beaters from outside the estate had to be paid at the end of each day.

Charlie Linge was an expert packer of game, which had to be packed into large wicker hampers and sent to Thetford station in time for the 8 a.m. train to Norwich. These were addressed to Messrs

The Head Keeper's Lodge into which Tom Turner and his family moved in 1919. Built from the local flint and with a slated roof, it was a more modern house than the one at Icklingham from which they moved.

G. and R.G. Bagshaw, Game Dealers, Norwich. I learned from Charlie the skills required in game larder work, often by example. I found he could pack hampers much quicker than I could.

The hampers we had to load on to the 'square cart', specifically built with round uprights along each side to allow air to circulate when it was full of game or rabbits.

The first time I drove to Thetford there was a piercing north-east wind. The load consisted of two tiers of three hampers and a front tier of two hampers. To drive I had to sit on the second tier of hampers at the front, with the top layer of the second tier at my back. I recall that on my arrival at the station loading ramp the porters helped me to unload and take the hampers across the line to catch the train to Norwich. Whilst this was going on a railway driver with his waggon and two horses was waiting to unload, and he swore at me for being in his way. As soon as I could I made for home; the open heathland on each side of the road afforded me no shelter from the cold wind.

Each afternoon I had to drive the cart to fetch rabbits from the warreners. One afternoon Dad told me to go down a track in the middle of Lakenheath Warren. I shall never forget that journey. It had been misty all morning, and when I set out the fog was getting thicker and I had difficulty in finding the track. The warren is an immense area, and with the fog becoming dense I realized I was lost. I kept on hopefully, and to my great relief I heard voices. The warreners had heard the muffled sounds of the horse and cart and had come to meet me.

The rabbits were soon hung over the short larch poles placed across the cart for this purpose. Then Fred Trett, always called Peter, biked ahead of me to guide me home. At that time he lived in a cottage at Old Elden, on the edge of the Warren; he later moved to Chalk Hall Farm with his wife and family.

Dad was much relieved when I arrived home. He recalled a time, some years before, when Allen Hill was Head Keeper at Elveden, that he had had to take some of his Icklingham men as beaters on to the Lakenheath Warren to 'drive in' as part of a shoot. The fog was dense on that occasion, and they had become completely lost until he saw a solitary tree which he recognised from the days when he was in charge of Sugarloaf Beat.

Soon after he had spotted the tree a message was passed down the line of beaters that the order had come from the Head Keeper to cancel the shoot, as neither guns nor beaters could see anything.

At the Works Yard, Mr. Evans, the Clerk of the Works, had had the estate carpenters build a low-sided body on to a Ford Model T chassis with the intention of using the vehicle instead of the horse-drawn carts previously used to convey building materials and the like about the estate. This body, if viewed from above, was L-shaped; it extended to the left of the driver to obtain extra loading length. The vehicle became known as 'The Matchbox'. Dad asked if he might borrow it to take the hampers to the station, and to my joy he gained permission. The driver was Charlie Palmer, a native of Lakenheath and brother-in-law to Jack Rutterford, the aviary keeper at the Hall. After a previous day's shoot, Charlie Linge and I would always be at the game larder early to pack the hampers ready for a 7.30 a.m. departure in order to catch the 8 a.m. train at Thetford. In the days of horse transport it would take a half-hour to get to the station.

Charlie Palmer always wore a hooded trenchcoat, since there was no cover for the driver. He told me that sitting on the hard, cold and often damp seat had given him piles! As a result he felt unwell and was often late. Each time this occurred Dad would consult his watch and remark that there was no sign of 'The Matchbox'. When Charlie at last arrived Dad would meet him, once again looking at his watch and saying, 'You're late, Charlie, you'll miss the train!'

Charlie was always polite. 'I can get to Thetford Station in a quarter of an hour,' he would say. This was the difference in time between horse transport and motor transport, with which my father could never come to terms.

Horses were still being used extensively at this time, but for the first few months at Elveden we had to manage without the groom, Mr. William Alderton, who had enlisted in the Suffolk Regiment and served on the Western Front at Ypres and in other war-torn areas. After the Armistice Bill returned home unscathed, and was then given the task of breaking in and training a young mare for driving or riding. His headquarters were at Summerpit Farm, and he revelled in the job. After this work was completed Bill returned to the Game Department.

The horses which used to pull the game van had been requisitioned for war work. A Thetford horse dealer was requested to bring out a suitable pair of black horses for inspection. Mr. Dow, the Estate Agent, came to the Game Department and watched Bill examine the pair very carefully. He pronounced them satisfactory, and a deal was struck. The horses were used for the next shoot.

With Mr. Alderton back, I had more time to devote to my office and game larder work. Meanwhile the horse I had been using for the Game Department had been taken back on to the Farms, so the Estate Office advertised for a suitable replacement and a dealer from Thetford brought one for us to see. Mr. Alderton examined the horse, which had also been in the war on the Western Front. It seemed to fit our needs, and the estate bought it; we named the mare Polly. One day I was driving along a cart track near Contract Wood when the horse suddenly fell down, but was up again instantly. We heard later that this horse had suffered shell-shock.

By this time Bagshaws, the game dealers, had purchased their own van and were able to collect the game. Charlie and I used to count the 'cold' birds into heaps of fifty, pheasant cocks and hens, and English and French partridges. Hares we used to leave hanging so that they could be counted in situ. When Bagshaws' van arrived at the larder we would carry five birds in each hand. The vehicle was soon loaded and the driver, who had packed them, said how many he had counted in. Two less than *our* tally!

This was more than Charlie could bear. 'Have the buggers off!' he shouted. I watched him and the driver unload; this time *our* total was agreed! The driver, a typical Norfolk man, said to me, 'Yew know yar job!' I handed him a pair of rabbits, which the Estate Office had agreed I could do.

As there was high unemployment after the First World War, Lord Iveagh decided that if the unemployed men from Thetford walked to the Elveden game larder once a week, they could buy a pair of rabbits for one shilling. We had to stipulate that they only came on Thursday afternoons, and I had to tie a rope barrier across the larder entrance to stop the men crushing in and starting to pick their own. I had to weigh each rabbit and write a cash sale ticket for each one.

After a fortnight I found a large, gaudy ice cream van was waiting around the corner. It seemed that the Thetford men had been taking their rabbits to him, he skinned the rabbits, kept the skins and handed the rabbits back. Good rabbit skins were making anything up to a shilling each at that time.

Later that year the Thetford police raided his establishment, and he was fined for making ice cream under dirty conditions and banned from trading.

That was not the only problem I had to cope with. When a shoot had finished at Elveden, the beaters all wanted to buy rabbits after they had been paid. One man in particular would start calling out in a loud voice, 'Save one for me, Dr. Cowan said I must always have some food in my stummick!'

There was another occasion when a large, loud-voiced man strode around the corner and walked into the larder, where I was sorting some game. I noticed his breath smelled strongly of whisky. He ordered six pheasants, then said, 'I might as well have four more.' I told him the price and expected cash, but he said 'I'll toss you, double or quits for this lot!' I hesitated, for it was a temptation, then I remembered I could not afford to lose. 'They are not my birds to gamble with, please pay me!' I told him, whereupon he produced a thick wad of notes and paid up.

I heard later that my 'customer' was a bookie, and he had come from Hockwold, where three days of hare coursing had taken place. After he had left, Mr. Alderton came across the yard, grinning, and said to me, 'You won't be here much longer, Ted, that man told me he was a personal friend of Lord Iveagh, and he would tell him to give you the sack.' I said, 'I'm ready to risk that, he tried to do me out of a lot of money!'

I also had to sell 'broken birds' which had been damaged in the shooting field. The best of these were sold at two shillings each, but some were too badly damaged to fetch that price. A customer who was renowned for liking a bargain was a Mrs. Hooks, who at that time used to live in a large room at the Water Tower and cooked for a number of single gardeners who lodged there. Mrs. Hooks would buy six or eight badly damaged birds and, after carefully cleaning and preparing them, turn them into tasty pies. She also knew which were the doe rabbits, so she was sure to obtain a tender one.

Another of my regular customers was Mr. David Manning, the Redneck Farm foreman, who would often bike to the larder during

The author, on left, collecting rabbits from the warreners. Beside him is James Layte, and the man with the gun is Fred Trett, who on one occasion guided the author home through the fog.

the lunch hour. On one occasion the demand had been such that I had sold out of damaged birds, so I offered him two old but undamaged cocks, which were heavy and would go for two shillings each. David thought it over, then said 'I had better go back and ask the wife.' Later he came back and said no.

In mid-November the Estate Office sent us the Christmas list for gifts of game to be sent away, which included the quantities and the names of those who should receive them first. Named and numbered labels were also sent.

Charlie and I had to reserve sufficient game from a big shoot. The following morning, after dispatching the rest to Norwich, we set about our task.

Some birds were packed and stitched into frail baskets (flat woven straw bags), and labelled. Charlie was adept at this task, using a sack needle and string. Others for local distribution were tied at the neck with white string and also labelled. Charlie sorted the labels and noted the names with great interest. 'Ah,' he would say, 'Mrs. Kerr Pearce, we must send this one some good birds, she's a good old lady!' This lady was the late Lady Iveagh's sister.

Working at this task on the long bench in the larder, your hands and feet became very cold. We were glad to be able to pop into the game office occasionally to warm ourselves at the open fire which Charlie had blazing away. My sister May would bring me a cup of cocoa, but Charlie would sometimes disappear on his bike, to return before long with a cheerful 'That's better, Teddy, a pint of old has warmed my old feet a treat!' When we had sown up all the bags we had to carry them to the Post Office.

Another important presents list which we used to deal with was that from the Rt. Hon. Col. Walter Guinness, M.P. These birds were selected from a December shoot, and were sent to those people in his constituency who had held a Conservative Association post for at least 12 months. Usually a brace each.

Occasionally this would coincide with the second distribution of the Estate's presents list. We had to estimate the numbers that might be required, keep these back from a Christmas shoot, and hope for the best. On one occasion we had not saved enough young cocks for our needs, so had to look at the old cocks to make up the numbers. Charlie looked at their long spurs and said 'This one was about here in the Prince's time!', a reference to the Maharajah Duleep Singh. With great skill he shortened the spurs with his knife to make them appear to be young cocks; certainly they were heavy birds! These also had to be distributed locally; one recipient had been a Liberal supporter the previous year!

Another thing I had to keep track of was the two brace of pheasants required for each gun on the last day of the three-day shoot. If these were not handed out on the shooting field, it was my job to get them to the Hall on Friday morning. Sometimes Mr. Harris, the butler, would ring up and say that a certain gun was leaving early, and I then had to bike down with the pheasants and leave them under the porch at the front door, where the cars assembled before departure. The butler would ensure that the gift was put into the right car. Woe betide me if I was slightly late!

At six o'clock one dark, cold morning Dad woke me up to say he had roused at four o'clock and was thinking about the 'marking out' he had done the previous day. Apparently he had put the sticks (where the guns would stand) in the correct places but had given the numbers (numbered cards) to a new keeper on the beat to place in the sticks overnight so that the cards did not get wet or disturbed in any way. He had suddenly remembered that he had not told his new man to put the card number one to the right when facing the drive, so off I had to go, furnished with another set of cards, in case I needed them.

My bicycle lamp casting a small beam ahead of me, I rode along the Turnpike (what we now call the A11), through Gibson's Lodge gateway, where the young keeper lived, on past Rakebottom to Howe Hill. I walked into the wood where the sticks had been placed, sure enough the cards were placed from left to right, so I removed them and put them in the correct sequence. I was back home in time for larder work after a round trip of some twelve miles! I never heard if anyone saw me.

The Estate Office had a special arrangement with the chemist in King Street, Thetford, with regard to the supply of poison. When required I had to bike down with a permit to collect a quantity of strychnine, for which I had to sign.

On my return to the game office, Dad would soon begin powdering these deadly crystals on the office table with his everyday pen-knife. He would then pick up the powder with the blade and transfer it into his 'poison' bottle, which he always carried in the breast pocket of his livery. I watched him with some trepidation, and later would pick up any crystals which had fallen on to the office floor. I also insisted that he washed his hands; I would open the door for him so that he did not contaminate the door knob! Whenever he used it on his beat, he would write 'poison' on a piece of card to warn people of its presence. He had used strychnine in his work from the age of eighteen, and thank goodness he never came to any harm. Another task I had during March was to mix arsenic with measured quantities of meal and sugar, with my bare hands, in a mixing bowl kept for this purpose. Dad told me the exact quantities to use. The mixture would then be transferred into stout bags ready to be used; the poison would be put down using an old dessert spoon, tied to a hazel stick.

The author outside the game office at Elveden about 1923.

One day I happened to mention in the Estate Office that I had been mixing rat poison. Mr. Charles Price said, 'I have been told that arsenic can be absorbed into the system from under your fingernails, and can build up to dangerous levels!' Having been warned of the dangers, I wrote out an order there and then for a pair of thin leather gloves which I used from then on for protection. The gamekeepers from Eriswell and Icklingham were supplied with sufficient arsenic and material to mix their own. Dad told me that the old gamekeepers did not realize the danger of handling these poisons. One old keeper, James Horn, actually used to taste the mixture to see if it was strong enough, and then spit it out.

One day I noticed a hornet flying into the ventilator on the ridge of the game larder roof; further investigation revealed that a large nest was being constructed. I informed the Estate Office, and the Head

Gardener from the Flower Gardens, a beekeeper, was sent to inspect the nest. His nickname was 'Blinky', due to his habit of snapping his eyelids. He spoke in a strong Norfolk dialect.

Blinky confirmed that there was a large nest in the ventilator. There was a narrow pathway on that side of the game larder, bounded by an iron railing erected to prevent anyone falling down the sheer cement wall next to it which had been built to prevent the larder walls from sliding into the large chalk pit near the edge of which the larder stood. Blinky borrowed a short ladder to reach the rain troughing that ran the length of the roof, then used an implement to reach up to the ventilator to clear a space for the poison which he wished to administer. He wrote out an order for the poison he needed, signed it as a beekeeper, and asked me to bike into Thetford to fetch it. I told the chemist that it was to destroy a hornets' nest on a roof.

'Rather you than me!' said the chemist as I departed.

On my return Blinky mixed the poison he required and then mounted the ladder. He wore gloves to protect his hands but nothing over his face. He told me that hornets flew straight at you, but if you could dodge them they would fly straight on and away from you. From a safe distance I watched as he dodged hornet after hornet, exclaiming 'You beggar!' in his deep Norfolk accent. He stood for ages with both hands holding the spraying apparatus that he was using to apply the poison; the hornets were beginning to roll down the roof and into the gutter. When at last he decided he had done a good job and was ready to leave I thanked him warmly, for I well knew he had relieved us of a great nuisance!

The next morning I used the same ladder to inspect the guttering. It was full to the top with dead hornets, and there were also quite a number in the guttering on the other side of the building.

Family matters 11

TWO years after we had all moved to the Headkeeper's Lodge my brother Russell, who was apprenticed to learn poultry keeping at Chivers Farm in Cambridgeshire, found his health failing and he had to come home. His nerves were in a bad state, and so on some mornings Mr. Alderton would take Russell out with him on his travels around the Estate to aid his recovery.

Mr. Alderton, who was much later to become my father-in-law, used to drive the Bank cart (so called because of the weekly trip to the bank to pay in or withdraw cash for office use) to Thetford every Thursday. The Estate Office clerks took turns to go with their wives. One day Charlie Price was chatting during the journey.

'I suppose if I was attacked, you would help me?'

'My job is to look after the horse!' Mr. Alderton replied.

'I suppose you think you're not paid to look after the cash?'

'Well,' replied Mr. Alderton, 'it's your job to look after the cash, and I don't suppose you'd stay in your present job if there wasn't any cash?'

'Oh well!' said Mr. Price, 'I must admit you're right!'

The next week he took Mr. and Mrs. Levick. Mrs. Levick sat in front beside Mr. Alderton, and her husband sat on the back seat. Presently Mrs. Levick's head drooped on to Mr. Alderton's shoulder as she fell fast asleep.

'Wake her up!' said Mr. Levick.

'That's quite all right,' said Mr. Alderton, 'I expect the sleep will do her good.'

At just about the time Russell came back home the *Bury and Norwich Post* sent their representative to the Game Yard to enquire if someone would act as their agent to receive their papers on Friday mornings and distribute them. This seemed something that would occupy Russell's thoughts, and with the job came a small monthly income. Russell agreed to take it on, and I told him I could sell most of the papers when people came to buy rabbits.

There was an old railway carriage in the big hatching pen in Lime Kiln Wood, and we cleared it out and made it habitable for a few hens so that Russell could start to practise the things he had been taught at Chivers Farm.

Whilst I was busy in the game office, my sister May was coping in the house. I often heard her singing songs which I found out later she was practising for a Women's Institute concert, having recently joined the Elveden branch. My younger sister, Dorothy, was also living at home.

One Easter Dad invited his London cousins, Lizzie and her husband, George Layfield, and Annie Traish, to stay with us over the Easter weekend. On Easter Saturday morning I drove to Thetford station to meet them. Having placed Annie and Liz beside me and George in the back, I started for home. All went well until I was descending Redneck Hill, when my horse fell flat but was up again instantly. I had my feet well extended and braced on the footboard and remained in my seat, but Annie and Liz left their seats and landed in a heap against the footboard. Happily they were not hurt, and we all arrived safely in time for dinner, which May had prepared.

On Easter Sunday the weather was very hot and our visitors sat in the shade of the great silver spruce at the bottom of the garden. Mid-morning May's young man, Bert Bailey, arrived to be introduced, and he invited George to go and have a drink at the beer house situated on the Brandon Road, run by the two Brown sisters. This was always known as 'Fanny Brown's', after one of the sisters. It exists today as The Elveden Inn. When we all sat down to lunch they had still not returned, so we waited a short while and then began our meal without them.

Later we heard a shuffling at the front door, and there was George being supported by Bert, who explained he thought the heat had been too much for George. Bert helped George down the garden path and on to a chair in the shade, where he remained for two hours! Liz was worried to see him in that condition, when he should have ben enjoying his Sunday dinner. We later heard from George that someone had laced his drink, which had made him helpless; normally he drank only beer.

Soon after our guests returned to London, cousin Liz was crushed against a wall by a car which had mounted the pavement, and she died a few days later in hospital. Sadly George was left alone with two young daughters to bring up.

Mr. Levick, the chief clerk at the Estate Office, had suggested to me that he would like to see reports of Elveden news sent to the *Thetford and Watton Times*. Thus it was that I began to write for the press. One of my early reports, I remember well, was the wedding between Mrs. Hooks' only daughter, Grace, and her fiance, Mr. Rimmington, from London. I knew Mr. Rimmington because he drove an ancient open-topped car that had tiller steering and used to go banging along the road as it headed for Budden's Garage, where my brother Arthur used to work as a mechanic. He told Arthur that if any parts rattled off his car he would stop and throw them in the back and fix them later!

Mr. Rimmington was a schoolmaster and worked out, using an algebraic formula, how many spokes Arthur would need to use when building a cycle wheel. Not that Arthur needed to be told.

I reported the wedding and then went to Mrs. Hooks' house with a bill for a special notice I had previously placed in the paper on her behalf. Whilst there, I inquired if she had liked my report of her daughter's wedding.

'Well,' she said, 'you know the biggest room in the world, I suppose?' I said, 'No.'

'It's the room for improvement!' she said.

Soon after this there was a serious accident at Elveden crossroads between a car and a Salvation Army van. The Salvation Army captain was so seriously injured that the doctor in attendance requested that the patient be carried into Mr. and Mrs. Collings' house, West Lodge, which stood nearby. Mrs. Collings provided a bed, and the doctor and the local nurse visited daily until the crisis was past.

I went to get details for my report to send to the newspaper, and afterwards I said how pleased I was to hear of the Salvation Army man's excellent recovery. Mrs. Collings said, 'I told him to trust in God and keep his bowels open!' Now her husband was an ex-soldier, and that sounded like an old army expression to me!

As motor traffic increased on the London Road (now the A11), the R.A.C. had a telephone box installed at the Elveden crossroads. A. patrol officer was stationed there and would salute cars bearing their badge and direct traffic when required.

A child named Janet, daughter of Walter and Mary Wood, who lived at the Crossroads, would come to the roadside and wave to the patrolman, and he would then cross the road and take her over to his side for a chat. One sad day the patrolman saw the little girl step into the road to come across to him and at the same time he spotted a fast car approaching. Instantly he dashed over the road to try and save the child, but both were hit by the car and killed.

One evening I heard of a serious accident between two cars at the Crossroads, and I telephoned the *Thetford and Watton Times* to ask them if they wanted a report. 'These car accidents are getting far more common, was there anyone killed?' I was asked. When I said there wasn't I was told 'Forget it!'

Early in 1922 the Annual Parochial Church Meeting was held in the church vestry, and as a local reporter I decided to attend. I found the new incumbent, the Rev. Selwyn Sharp, in the chair.

I was taking notes as the meeting proceeded, and it was mentioned that there was a vacancy for a sidesman. Two or three proposals were made, but the Rector said, 'I should like to see some young faces, I noticed Reg Blower was in church Sunday morning and I was going to propose him, but we cannot elect him in his absence, so I therefore propose Mr. Edward Turner, being the only young person here!' I was duly elected.

The next morning I saw Mr. William Levick in the Estate Office. He congratulated me on my appointment and said, 'I don't suppose you will ever be wanted.'

That same spring I reported the death of Miss Annie Manning, who had held the post of Treasurer to the Parochial Church Council. She was the eldest of the large family of Mr. and Mrs. David Manning. I was asked by Mr. Levick if I would replace her as Treasurer, and I held this post for many years.

The first time I biked to the Hall on some errand I went into the courtyard and climbed the great steps up to the luggage entrance. I looked to the right, then to the left, and decided to go left. The first thing I noticed was the extreme heat which prevailed; I had just left the very cold game larder!

My decision to go in this direction was justified as I found Mr.

The Turner family and some of the Wright family photographed at Head Keeper's Lodge, Elveden, about 1920.
In the back row, left to right, are the author, Hilda Wright, brother Ian Turner, father Tom Turner, brother Russell Turner, Elsie Constance Wright, brother Arthur Turner. Seated in front are Dorothy Turner, Olive Wright, David and Florence Wright, Freda Wright and Frances May Turner.

William Speed, who readily put me right on many things I was uncertain about. On future occasions he would hail me and have a few words; his advice was always helpful, especially when he told me to come up the steps to the side door and from there to go down some more steps to the gun room, where I often needed to go.

Lord Iveagh's London household from 5 Grosvenor Place used to come by train to Thetford Station at the beginning of the shooting season and remain at Elveden Hall until after Christmas. As soon as they were all in residence I received orders from the Chef, an Italian named de Luca. He always wanted morels, puff balls and watercress, pheasants and English partridges.

He knew from experience that one of King George V's favourite dishes was English partridge pudding. The Chef had been in Lord Iveagh's employ for a number of years, but by the time I met him he seldom left his room; he wrote the menus and his trained kitchen staff could do all the cooking.

He always shouted at everyone. I was greeted with a loud 'Boy!', then given a list of items and the day he wanted them.

When he died he was replaced by a French chef named M. Coumiege, who proved somewhat temperamental. One day he gave me an order for pheasants which, as usual, I delivered and placed on the marble shelves in the large larder. I had no difficulty in selecting the best young cock pheasants, but I had not had much experience with young hen pheasants. I decided to send some with good plump breasts; later on I learned much more about the special colour of their legs which is the secret of a good hen bird.

Later in the day I went to the Hall on some other mission. When I got there Mr. William Speed told me the Chef wanted to see me. I went across to the other corridor, slowly opened the kitchen door and closed it behind me. Standing with my back to the door, I saw the Chef near the place where 'Kitchen George' was working. Next moment the Chef saw me; he snatched up a carving knife and, brandishing it above his head and shouting at the top of his voice, rushed across the kitchen towards me. I looked him straight in the face and tried to collect my thoughts; I was tempted to hit him in the midriff with my clenched fist, but decided against it. The Chef grabbed me by my left arm, dragged me to the top of the steps which led down to the larder, rushed down the steps and came back up clutching some of the hen pheasants, which I could see had already been cooked. Still shouting at the top of his voice, he yelled, 'I said YOUNG!' at the same time hurling the offending birds to the floor one by one. Having repeated the action half a dozen times he released his grip. I could only say I was sorry and that I would not let it happen again!

Not long after this incident I had to go to the kitchen with more game. The kitchen staff told me that the Chef wanted me. I wondered what he needed me for this time. They directed me back into the corridor; nearly opposite the kitchen door I saw an open door to a small room, and inside, there was the Chef on his knees, crying.

I said, 'You wanted me, Sir?' 'BOY! How you spell ELVEDEN?' The cause of his disturbed state of mind was that he had been asked to make a 21st Birthday Cake for Lord Elveden; an enormous iced cake was already there before him, but nobody there could or would spell Elveden. I spent an hour with him as he skilfully fashioned the letters in icing sugar.

When it was finished he seemed completely exhausted. It was certainly a lovely cake to look at, but I had no opportunity to taste it! This experience confirmed my opinion that M. Coumiege was a very temperamental person.

Whenever I went to see the Chef I came up the stairs just inside the side door which people used as a handy entry into the kitchen; this was in the old servants' quarters which have since been demolished.

I was always fascinated to watch George Cain, 'Kitchen George' as he was known, with his bare arms and light leather apron, at his task of cleaning the massive copper pans and boilers. He had enormous pride in his work, never looked up from his task and seldom spoke to anyone; when he did it was quite obvious that he was a cockney. He used white sand to scour the pans and boilers, and they came up bright and shiny.

Kitchen George's work began at breakfast, and continued after lunch and after dinner, which was at 8 p.m. George's one half-day off was on a Thursday, when he would emerge from his room looking extremely smart, wearing a bowler hat and overcoat and carrying a walking stick, to go for a walk in the Park and enjoy the fresh air.

Whenever a deer was killed during a shoot, the Chef would ask for

The author's brother Arthur married Elsie Constance Wright at Icklingham on 20th September, 1924. Afterwards the bride and groom with all the main guests posed outside the church for this photograph; they are sitting and standing in The Street, which forms part of the main road from Bury St. Edmunds to Mildenhall. Standing at the back are, left to right, two unknown friends of the family, the author, another unknown friend, Russell Turner, Aunt Ginny, Tom Turner's sister, another unknown friend, Sam Atkins, and at right, wearing his medals, Charles Jarrold. Charles's brother, George Jarrold, stands with arms crossed at left. In the middle row are Frances May Turner, Roy Budden, Olive Wright, Ian Turner, Arthur and his bride, Freda Wright and Olive Dorothy Turner, and seated in front are Tom Turner, Hilda Wright and Mr and Mrs. David Wright.

it to be sent to the Hall kitchen. The correct method was to hang it in the game larder, head down, to cool overnight, allowing the blood to settle in the ribcage. The next evening Harry Fuller, the shepherd who lived at Chalk Hall, would walk down to the larder in order to flay the deer and to cut it into the portions the Chef required.

Dissecting the carcase at the joints was a fine art. The skin had no value, but the blood had sometimes to be saved, as was the 'pluck' (heart, liver and lungs). Harry was a cheerful soul, ready to chat and smile while he worked. One day as he worked Harry said 'How many cars do you think I saw go past Chalk Hall last Bank Holiday?' 'I have no idea,' I said. 'Well,' said Harry, 'I counted eleven in the morning, and ten came back in the evening!' Because I had to type the shoot programmes I always knew in advance when His Majesty King George V was coming to Elveden Hall. When I had to go to the Hall in the early morning, I used to see the staff from the kitchen gardens bringing in the vegetables for the Chef. The staff from the flower gardens would also be busy arranging flower decorations.

On occasions I would meet the housemaids as they marched in formation to the Servants' Hall for breakfast. One morning, one of the maids said, 'Hello Ted, how's your leg?' I blushed as I realized that I was limping from a twisted knee sustained whilst playing cricket. I thanked her and said it was improving, then she said, still marching, 'Where do you get that rosy colour in your cheeks?' 'Oh,' I said, 'Fresh air and cold water!'

At the top end of that corridor was Mrs. Morris' room. Mrs. Morris, the Housekeeper, was extremely efficient and very strict with the housemaids. Sharing this room was the late Lady Iveagh's lady's maid. They and the butler, Mr. Harris, always took their meals in this room and were waited upon. At the top end of the other corridor was the butler's room and pantry.

Mr. Harris had a loud voice, and would not hesitate to inform me if I had not carried out my instructions properly. As butler, he was in charge of the four or five parlour maids and other servants.

Living in the Old Rectory at this time was Lord Iveagh's private secretary, Mr. C.H. Bland, and his family. When Mr. Bland moved to Lord Iveagh's London residence his son Donald, who had been put in charge of the Woods Department, occupied the Old Rectory with his young French wife Gaby (short for Gabrielle), whom he had married while serving in France during the war.

Mr. Alderton had to go to the Old Rectory one day to pick up the housekeeper, Mrs. Skeet, and young Mrs. Bland to take them into Thetford. They had just passed the Thetford Gap when the horse shied and reared at the same time; both ladies threw their arms around Mr. Alderton's neck. Needless to say, he had great difficulty in controlling the horse, not to mention himself, I should think!

Mr. Alderton's daughter, Miss Marjorie Alderton (whom I worshipped from afar, and who was to be my future wife, although neither of us knew it then), had been installed as a clerk to the Clerk of the Works department, and Donald Bland used another desk in the same office. One Saturday morning, after paying out the wages, he found he was ten shillings short.

He checked everything very carefully, and came to the conclusion that one of his men named Dimmy Neal had been overpaid. On Monday morning Donald went to see Dimmy, who had indeed received the ten shillings.

Donald spoke to him sharply. 'Why did you keep the money?' he wanted to know.

Dimmy was unrepentant. 'When I'm short, I tell you — when you're short, you tell me.'

Near Christmas time the eagerly awaited Servants' Ball was held at the Hall, in the large dining room. The butler, Mr. Harris, issued invitations on behalf of His Lordship to those who were eligible to attend. The staff were allowed to invite a friend.

On the evening of the Ball the Family dined early so as to give the staff time to clear the dining room and polish the floor before positioning chairs around the room for the guests. This done, the staff retired to dress for the evening.

A band from Cambridge was engaged, and at the appointed time struck up with the Sir Roger de Coverley. The butler and housekeeper led off the dancing, and dancing then went on unabated until the supper interval was called. The guests lined up in pairs and processed along the long corridor to the servants' hall.

I asked Miss Alderton to accompany me, but being very shy did not walk close enough for her to take my arm. The village constable, who loved to tease people, was close behind us. 'You're pulling away from the pole, get in nearer!' he told me, referring to a pair of carriage horses, one of which would try to pull away from the centre pole. I sat beside Marjorie for supper.

When all the guests were seated, Lord Iveagh, sitting in a wheel-chair, took his place at the head of the table, flanked by the Rectors of the three parishes and office staff with their wives. After the loyal toast, a few speeches were made, followed by grace, whereupon eating began in earnest, with plenty of good wine to wash the food down. Afterwards dancing was resumed with renewed vigour.

When it was all over Marjorie joined her parents and I walked home with them. It had been a thoroughly enjoyable evening.

Cricketing memories 12

AS THE winter months elapsed my thoughts turned to the onset of the cricket season. My father knew I had had a hard season in the game larder and office and therefore encouraged me to try to join the local boys in an early practice. With this in mind I biked to the Fire Station gates and slowly free-wheeled downhill, stopping with my right hand resting on the balustrade in front of the Hall pond.

Patiently I waited. Soon I heard voices as two cyclists swung into view and continued rapidly on the footpath leading to the cricket pitch. A voice called out to me, 'Are you coming down?' That was like music to my ears.

I left my position and biked after them, down the hill to the cricket ground. Their first objective was to get a cricket net out of the long wooden box situated near the belt of trees, and I helped them to erect it. To my surprise Reg Blower said to me, 'You can have first knock,' and handed me a bat.

Watching me take my stance, he remarked to Frank Graver, 'A left-hander, have we got one in our side?' A few more players joined us, and all had a go at the nets.

One of the early fixtures was against Barnham, a neighbouring village. One of our senior players, C. Spruce, used to transport some of the gear in a small light van pulled by one horse, while the younger players cycled carrying bats and that sort of thing.

The Barnham ground was near North Farm. At one end there was a pond that sometimes contained a considerable amount of water if there had been recent rain. As the match proceeded the ball ran into the pond twice, but I was able to hold two catches. When Elveden batted I succeeded in scoring eight runs.

Some of our early batsmen partially failed, but in the end we won by a small margin.

In the 1920s the most successful team in our area was the Heath House eleven from Brandon. We were always keen to get a regular fixture with them.

On the Saturday we were expecting to go to Brandon a terrific thunderstorm broke at Elveden, with torrents of rain. We had given up any hopes of cricket after that! About 10 a.m. I heard the telephone ring, and the message from Brandon was, 'Very fine here, shall expect you,' so we duly travelled in the Game Department shooting van to Brandon. Our captain, the Rev. John Selwyn Sharp, who was then Rector of Elveden, travelled by car.

The Heath House ground was owned by Mr. A.W. Rought-Rought, who had made a fortune from his rabbit skin factory. So much so that his three sons were able to go to Cambridge, and two of the sons, Basil, a left-handed batsman, and Rodney, a fast bowler who came within a shade of being selected for the England team, played for the University.

Because of a twisted knee, I had to take the post of scorer on this occasion. Our newly elected captain lost the toss, and Brandon elected to bat, Wilfred Bowers opening the bowling. The first ball to the left-handed batsman bowled him for a duck. Soon the other opener was dismissed and joined the left-hander near the scoring table. The Elveden attack and good fielding dismissed Heath House for fifty-four runs.

The Elveden innings got off to a good start, Bowers and Frank Graver scoring freely. Reg Blower had a good knock, and we scored a total of seventy-eight.

As the Heath House players dejectedly left the field, our captain met Mr. Rought-Rought and said, 'Awfully glad we beat you!' 'Served us right for getting out for fifty-four!' was his reply.

Another match against Heath House was at Elveden on our new ground, in the Park, on top of the hill. I was told by Wilfred Bowers and Frank Sharp, who had played there, that the first Elveden cricket pitch was situated in the meadow in front of Chalk Hall Farm.

Heath House were batting, and again Wilfred Bowers had captured some early wickets. Their captain, Mr. Rought-Rought, decided to promote himself in the batting order to try to knock Wilfred off his length. He received the first ball and, leaving one foot in the batting crease, stepped forward an enormous stride so he could not move, missed the ball, heard it hit his wicket, and roared, 'BLA-A-A-ST!' at the top of his voice. I was fielding at point and was able to join in Wilfred's delight! This was probably the only time we beat them at Elveden.

Once again on a beautiful hot day at Elveden, Basil the left-hander opened the innings. Accomplished batsman as he undoubtedly was, he dealt skilfully with our attack and, fielding at my usual position of point, I was kept very busy. He had reached the eighties when he drove a ball at catchable height straight at me.

I felt it strike the side of one hand, then I dropped it! I felt like crawling under the pitch. Nevertheless, we enjoyed the match as always. We knew we could not expect to win very often.

On another occasion the younger son, Desmond, was bowling at me. My priority was to guard my stumps. To my surprise ball after ball sped past my legs, so I decided it was time I tried to hit them; the sixth ball curved round on to my off stump — I saw it all the way, but my defence was too late!

As our cricket fixtures settled into an annual shape I received a surprise invitation from Didlington Hall. I had read in the press that they had already played at Heath House, and they also said they had not lost a match for one and a half seasons. Our club decided to take them on. We won the toss, opting to bat. Several good innings resulted in the useful total of one hundred and twenty-four runs.

We took the field, and gradually wickets fell. In due time their total topped the one-hundred mark, and soon their score came to within four of our own. The last man in but one skied the ball, and at my position at point I had an anxious wait, but was very relieved when I caught it.

Tension was mounting on both sides as the last man came in. He showed his intention by running up the pitch and dispatching the ball for four. The scores were now level! He tried the same method with the next ball but the bowler, Charlie Flack, banged the ball in short and hard. It bounced over the batsman and hit the stumps!

In a subsequent match with Didlington Hall one of their batsmen proved to be a giant of a man. Indeed, he towered above Arthur Flack, one of our bowlers, who was quite a small man. When he walked to the wicket the batsman gazed across to the copper dome of Elveden Hall, some five hundred yards away, and said, jokingly, 'What will I score if I put the ball on top of the Hall?' He took guard, and Arthur Flack ran up to bowl. The batsman took an enormous swipe, missed, and was clean bowled!

When we visited Didlington we found their matting wicket difficult after being used to grass. They won the toss, and their opening pair put on one hundred runs, giving us plenty of exercise in the field. When our turn came to bat we put up a decent show, but failed to win.

One high spot of each season was the annual Whit Monday match, which normally started at twelve noon and went on until both sides had completed two innings each. The match was held at Elveden on the pitch on the top of the hill. The first opponents were Eriswell, but later on Icklingham took alternate years.

Early on the Monday morning the great tent, which Lord Iveagh used for his shooting parties, was erected on the north side of the cricket pitch. The tent accommodated both changing rooms, one at each end, and the catering facilities, tables for lunch and tea being set out in between the two changing rooms.

This particular season Eriswell were the visitors. Elveden won the toss and elected to bat, and Sam Atkins and I opened the innings. We knew the Eriswell bowlers were proud of their skills with the ball. I survived the first over all right, and then I watched Sam face his first ball. It was wide of the off stump; he tried to cut it, had a touch and was caught at first slip.

Wilfred Bowers was the next man in. He received a similar ball, also touched it and was caught at slip. Reg Blower followed, his third ball went through to the wicket keeper. The fourth ball and Reg also got a touch and was dispatched in the same way. With such a flying start, Eriswell dismissed us for thirty-nine runs.

After lunch had been taken we went out to field. The Eriswell team comprised William Lock (captain), Reg Hanslip, Fred Warby, the three Taylor brothers, Les Lock, Joe Heffer and three others whose names escape me. Elveden's regular bowlers were augmented by Frank Graver, who had left his employment on Elveden Estate but was home for Whitsuntide. Keen bowling and fielding curtailed the Eriswell total to seventy runs.

After tea had been taken, Elveden began their second innings, making a steady start until Frank Graver came in. Then the pace quickened, with some brilliant strokes as his score mounted to fifty not out. Elveden's final total was eighty-three runs.

Eriswell began their second innings facing a total of fifty-two to win. Once again Frank's bowling turned things in Elveden's favour, and we won by a narrow margin. Then the protests began! William Lock said we had no right to have Frank in our team; we said he had been born at

Members of Elveden Cricket Club. In the back row are Tom Trayes, William Graver, Monty Wells, Bert Atkins and the author. In the front row are Wilfred Bowers, Reg Flack, Sam Atkins, Reg Blower, Charles Flack, Fleming Dow and Edward Benstead.

Elveden and had played all his early days with us, and still remained a fully paid up club member, so that was the end of the matter! One Saturday afternoon we visited Icklingham. Elveden batted first and I, as opening batsman, realized that Ernest Atkins was about to bowl to me. The outfield was long and rough, and I knew there would no easy runs, but after two overs of watchful defence I managed a few singles. Ernie tried every trick he knew to get me out, but I countered successfully, and after several overs he had still failed to take my wicket.

Finally his captain changed the bowling. His successor immediately went round the wicket, and in his first over he knocked my off stump back. 'I always could get left-handers out!' he said triumphantly as I walked off. His name was George Nichols. I passed Ernie on my way off the field, and he said to me, 'You stubborn old bugger, you!'

Another Saturday afternoon at Icklingham and we had had some difficulty in amassing a full team. Finally Mr. Dow, the Elveden Estate Agent, came in his own car and brought with him young Tom Adams.

Icklingham batted first and set us a very respectable target to beat. When we batted our early wickets fell rather cheaply. Mr. Dow went in at number eight, and then another wicket fell. Last man in was young Tom Adams. Both batsmen employed some unusual methods, but runs began to flow quickly and some cheeky blows were struck. This exciting last wicket stand saved us the match.

There was a further most thrilling match against Eriswell, on their home ground. They had batted first and set us a target of sixty-eight runs. We began with a few early losses, including myself, but an exception was Reg Blower, who was in fine form. As he gradually ran out of partners he was on the fifty mark. Well down the batting order, my brother Ian joined Reg at the crease.

The suspense for the onlookers was becoming unbearable. Ian had spent his early years at Eriswell and knew both the pitch and his opponents well. Charlie Flack was seated on the grass just behind me as we watched from the boundary. He was too excited to watch and was pulling up great handfuls of grass as he listened to the shouts as Reg scored boundary after boundary.

Meanwhile Ian played as calmly as could be, making sure that Reg received most of the bowling, whilst contributing his own runs. Charlie kept saying to me, 'Have they bowled another ball yet?' Reg scored the winning hit with a magnificent boundary, and was undefeated when the game closed with a narrow margin in favour of Elveden.

I cannot miss out the only occasion when I had the pleasure of participating in an Elveden century. It happened on the Elveden ground when we met Thetford Town. We batted first, and Reg Blower and I opened the innings. I used my normal method of defence, whilst Reg was soon off the mark with his fine straight drives towards mid-off, and runs began to flow. Three times the power of his shots was such that the fielders dropped the catches!

Mine was the first wicket to fall, at seventy-two for one, of which I had contributed sixteen. Further batsmen played their part, and soon we passed the hundred mark. Reg went merrily on and finally reached one hundred and twenty-two runs!

The season came when we entertained Icklingham for the Whit-Monday all-day match. Early that morning we had had a severe thunderstorm with torrential rain, followed by bright sunshine, and we began to wonder what effect this would have on the pitch. There was also concern about the large tent which had been pitched just before the storm; when the Elveden players began to arrive they found the guyropes had tightened so much with the wet that they were unable to slacken them. The result was that suddenly there was a loud rending sound and the tent split apart about midway, but at least each end still provided some shelter.

The Icklingham team arrived, and we batted first in extreme heat. Our wickets fell like autumn leaves, and we were dismissed for twelve runs!

Lunch was then taken in the damaged tent, and over lunch we discussed the state of affairs. Before we took the field we knew that there must be something unusual in the wicket. Our bowlers got to work, and the Icklingham batsmen found the pitch just as tricky as we had. They were all out for thirteen runs. I recall that in the second innings Elveden won narrowly.

I had had several bruises and hard knocks during my time as a 'stone-waller', but the day we met Brandon Town at Elveden, that I shall never forget. Brandon batted first and scored about sixty runs. When we batted Tom Trayes opened with me. The third ball I received I stepped forward to meet it, but to my surprise it seemed to come straight up off the pitch and hit the right side of my head, just above my ear. I dropped my bat and fell almost unconscious at the crease. Tom Trayes and all the other players, including the bowler who was greatly concerned, rushed to pick me up.

I slowly recovered, and hoped I might be able to continue to bat, but Tom persuaded me to leave the field. He assisted me to walk to the tent. Soon I began to cry. I said to Tom, 'I feel like a kid who can't stop crying.' Tom said very kindly to me, 'It will do you good to cry, I've seen many wounded men crying on the battlefield.'

I was unable to resume my innings, and Tom stayed with me until the match was over. When all the other players had gone Wilfred Bowers biked up the field to see how I was. He told me he had just got to the iron fence on the side of the ground opposite the tent when he heard the ball hit my head; it sounded like a gunshot, he told me.

Tom went off with my thanks, and I said I thought I could ride my bike. Wilfred insisted he would see me home, though. By this time my head had taken on a dull ache. Having negotiated the driveway downhill, I had to walk slowly up the hill past the Hall before remounting my bike and riding home. Much to Wilfred's relief he saw me unlock the door and go in.

Dad was not at home, but I managed to make a cup of tea. Later that evening Wilfred called round to see how I was; I thanked him for his help and said I was feeling a little better. When my Dad came home later, I went to bed. During the night my head became very painful, and I called to my father who was in the next bedroom, but he did not hear me.

The next morning in the stable I saw Bill Alderton, my father-in-law to be. He was alarmed when I told him what had happened. The rest of the week I kept as quiet as I could, but on the Friday I biked down to the surgery at the Cross Roads to see Dr. Oliver senior. I told him that when I walked I felt strange pains in my head. He grasped my skull in both hands; he could not feel any sign of a fracture, he said, adding that there was no doubt I had been badly concussed and that most probably the nerves were just coming back to life. Fortunately I did not seem to suffer any long-term effects.

My cricket memoirs would not be complete without mention of a memorable day spent at Mr. Lionel Robinson's country seat at Old Buckenham Hall, Norfolk, where we watched the Australian visitors. My friend Bill Reeve joined me at my home at six on the morning of Thursday, 5th May, 1921, and we were picked up by a heavy lorry that was en route for North Walsham, Norfolk. That took us and our cycles to an appropriate spot on the A11, where we were put down to continue our journey on our bicycles. We soon noticed the flow of spectators going in the same direction.

We found a sheltered spot on the edge of the ground and ate our sandwiches while waiting for the start of play. This came when the bitter chill of that morning was still a hindrance, but we were treated to a fine show of batting by J.B. Hobbs, who retired hurt with his score at eighty-five, as well as a good all-round display of cricket by the Australian visitors.

At the close of play Bill and I set off for home on our cycles, having some difficulty with the traffic also using the same narrow road. By the end of our long journey we were both very tired, but glad we had succeeded in seeing the Australians!

Cricket had been played at Old Buckenham for very many years, but not, it seems, on Sundays. Looking at Volume one of *The Cricketer* which came out in that same year that Bill Reeve and I watched the Australians, I see that 'In November, 1817, several persons, who had long resisted the threats and entreaties of the inhabitants of Old Buckenham, were convicted before a magistrate at Larlingford, Norfolk, and fined for playing cricket on Sunday, 2nd October, on Old Buckenham Green.'

Mr. and Mrs. Abraham Sadler, who were married in 1890. Mrs. Clara Sadler was a remarkable lady and a wonderful character. Born in Greenwich in 1862, she came to Elveden to work for the Rev. St. George Walker. In 1897 they moved into a newly built cottage; her husband died in 1911, but she remained in the cottage for another forty-three years. Mrs. Sadler was a very kind lady with a sunny disposition and an artistic temperament; whenever a village concert was arranged she was one of the star performers. She had an excellent voice and a wonderful line in patter which would have her audience roaring with laughter. Mrs. Sadler also made tiny items of furniture from peacocks' feathers and satin.

Between the wars 13

IN NOVEMBER, 1921, when returning from an errand to the Hall, I began to feel ill. I fell off my bike when attempting to dismount, and struggled back on foot to the game office.

I sat on my chair for a while and began to feel even worse. I managed to drag myself into the house and asked my sister for some whisky, and she, realizing how ill I was, called the Nurse. When she arrived the Nurse told me that I had contracted rheumatic fever.

I was very ill for a long time, and it was not until Christmas that I was allowed my first piece of solid food, a tiny piece of yorkshire pudding! During this time I was in great pain and needed constant nursing — I was literally wrapped in cotton wool and confined to bed. It was a long time before I was allowed out of bed, and even longer before I was allowed downstairs.

One afternoon in January, 1922, I was in a heavy sleep on the sofa in the living room when my sister Maggie came in with her friend, Hilda Roper. I roused just in time to hear Hilda say, 'Don't he look bad!'

As the weeks went by I began to take short walks down the garden path, wearing an old railwayman's greatcoat which had belonged to my sister Maggie's boyfriend, Bert Bailey. I bought it from him for £1, and a tailor fitted an extra warm collar that I found gave me protection from the March winds.

Dad approached Mrs. Collings, who lived at West Lodge, at the end of the carriage drive, and asked her if she would allow me to rest there during my walk to the lodge and back. She agreed and said she would make me a cup of cocoa. One sunny March morning I set off with my walking stick, but I found my legs were still weak and the weight of my railway coat was too much for me. I was glad to knock at Mrs. Collings' door; when she opened it she fixed me with a piercing stare and said, 'My God! you do look bad!' She made me a large cup of cocoa, which I had some difficulty coping with.

While I was drinking she regaled me non-stop with village gossip. When I at last managed to take my leave, I thanked her and made my way slowly home. Maggie was worried because I had been away so long. When I mentioned all the scandal I had heard, Maggie told me the whole parish knew that weeks ago!

I continued to gather strength during March, and after a thorough examination Dr. Cowan gave me permission to resume light duties in the game office. His final words were 'Do not get cold or wet for a year!'

During my long absence from work Tom Trayes took over my duties at the game larder and office, and was an enormous help to my father.

It was a well-known fact that gamekeepers headed for Crufts Dog Show in Norwich at the end of the shooting season. In 1923 Mr. Adams, the traveller for Bagshaw's, the game dealers, invited Dad to go to the show with him. Dad declined the invitation, but suggested I might like to go in his place, so it was arranged that Mr. Adams would meet me at Norwich Thorpe Station and take me to the show.

On the day of the show I set off on my bike in time to catch the 8 a.m. train to Norwich, and arrived to find Mr. Adams waiting for me in his large car. We chatted whilst waiting for his other guests to arrive. To my surprise they turned out to Mr. Bill Bayfield, who used to be with Lord Iveagh at Elveden, and his younger brother, Hardy.

Off we went to the show, and we were soon visiting the various stands. Drinks were on offer at each stand and jokes began to be exchanged between the Bayfields — I knew from experience that Bill was always ready for a laugh. We came to the stand of Gaymers, the well-known Attleborough cider makers, and I had a small glass of cider with some biscuits, remarking how nice it was.

My companions urged me to ask for another glass, telling me that it was not intoxicating. Well, I did, and I noticed the look of surprise on the face of the Gaymer's representative as he handed it to me. After a few minutes the strong cider overcame me and I had to hold on to something for support, while the Bayfields roared with laughter.

We had arrived at the show rather late. I do not recall seeing any dogs, but I do recall that our host took us to a restaurant for a good meal. I began to worry about missing my train home, but Mr. Adams promised me that he would take me to the station in time. The Bayfields seemed to be in no hurry while there were drinks to be had, but at last we all set off for the station, and with much relief I boarded the train. It was, I realized, a much later train than the one I had hoped to catch.

I had the compartment to myself and shortly put my feet up and laid full length on the seat; within minutes I was fast asleep. I woke with a start, wondering where I was. Luckily Thetford was the next stop. I collected my bike from the Railway Tavern nearby, and then rode through the cold night the four miles home.

Dad had begun to worry because I was so late, so I recounted the day's events. He said laughingly, 'That's why I didn't want to go, I know what the Bayfields are like!'

On Saturday, 25th July, 1926, Elveden Cricket Club travelled by coach to Icklingham. On the way we all noticed the extreme heat that prevailed.

Icklingham batted first, and before they were all out a sharp thunderstorm broke out, followed by torrential rain. The players sheltered in a barn, and tea was taken early. Both captains agreed that with the pitch under water any further play was impossible, so our coach left for home, for which we were grateful as we all felt the heat was far too oppressive to play cricket.

After supper I went to bed, leaving the bedroom window open as usual. About four o'clock the next morning I was awakened by the many pheasants which were roosting in the trees around the house all shrieking in terror.

I then heard a distinct rumble which increased in volume to resemble the sound of a tube train approaching — I had heard it once on a trip to London — followed by the sensation that the 'undergound' was passing beneath our house, causing a continuous severe vibration. I lay still a little longer, then decided I would tell Dad, who was sleeping in the next room. 'What the devil do you think it could have been?' he asked. 'Well,' I said, 'it must have been an earthquake!'

Later that morning I followed my usual duty and took the dog out for a run. I went past the Hall and along the drive towards Grey Cottage, where Robert Ransome, the hall carpenter, lived.

I stopped and asked him, 'Did you feel your house shaking last night?' 'Yes,' he replied, 'a whole shelf of crockery in the kitchen was shot on the floor!' Mr. Ransome was pleased to hear that he wasn't the only one to have felt the tremor.

The same afternoon I cycled to Chalk Hall to interview the parents of Miss Grace Halls, in order to obtain a report for the *Bury Free Press* of their daughter's wedding, which had taken place the previous day. I spent some time asking all the usual questions, then I said, 'What did you think of the earthquake last night?' 'Earthquake?' they replied, 'we never felt anything here, we were too tired and slept very soundly!'

On 7th October,1927, we were informed that the First Earl of Iveagh had died at his London residence, 5 Grosvenor Place. On hearing the sad news the Clerk of the Works had to perform the task of opening the family vault in Elveden churchyard. Having opened it up he discovered that a great deal of water had accumulated since Lady Iveagh had been interred in February, 1916, and this had to be pumped out.

The funeral of the Earl, head of the Guinness brewing firm, naturally attracted attention in the newspapers, one of which reported how 'A farm cart, drawn by plough horses, conveyed the coffin, austere in its plain severity, to the church, where, with glittering crozier held aloft, the Bishop of St. Edmundsbury and Ipswich waited to perform the last rites.'

The paper particularly noticed how besides the Family there were 'black-coated officials from the estate offices, butlers, footmen and chauffeurs, gamekeepers, labourers in workaday clothing, serving women in neat black, and village children all showing a sign of mourning for the man who had their interests at heart.'

Soon after Dad had met the Second Earl and Countess of Iveagh, he mentioned to her ladyship that my sister Dorothy was looking for a job. Lady Iveagh promised she would think about this, and later

Dorothy was taken on, on a month's trial, as a nursery maid under Mrs. Sutherland, nanny to Lord and Lady Iveagh's son, Arthur, Lord Elveden, and their daughters, the Ladies Honor, Patricia and Brigid Guinness.

Lord Iveagh brought with him to Elveden a Private Secretary, Captain Waller, who had suffered multiple wounds in the Great War when he became trapped in some barbed wire entanglements and had been caught in machine-gun fire. His role was to entertain the guests when Lord and Lady Iveagh were occupied with Estate affairs.

During that season, Captain Waller requested that the short-barrelled guns belonging to the late Earl be taken to the Hall. These guns, which had been specially made for the late Earl by a gunmaker named Bond, of London, with curved stocks to accommodate the stoop which he developed with age, were always kept in the game office. I took them out of the glass-fronted cupboard and placed them in their protective covers, cycled to the Hall and entered past the Odd Man's door. I left the guns in the usual place for the Butler to take in to Lord Iveagh.

I had only just returned to the game larder when the telephone rang again and Captain Waller said sharply, 'Lord Iveagh and I are still waiting in the Cedar Room for you to bring the guns!' I said, 'I brought them half an hour ago and left them in the usual place outside the butler's door.'

'Lord Iveagh wants you to bring them into the Cedar Room!' Captain Waller replied, so I returned to the Hall, picked up the guns, and found my way to the Cedar Room and apologised. I then took off the covers and handed the guns to Lord Iveagh.

'Were there not three guns?' His Lordship asked me.

I said, 'I only know of these two, my Lord, but I will ask my father as soon as I get home.'

Although I knew where the missing gun was, I dare not tell Lord Iveagh in case it caused trouble. Lady Honor, his daughter, had borrowed the gun some time earlier. I left this problem for my father to sort out!

The annual Servants' Balls were popular events at Elveden, but, alas, all good things have an end. The Second Earl and Countess of Iveagh

Lord and Lady Iveagh

request the pleasure of

Mr & Mrs Alderton & Mr Alderton

Company at Servants' Ball

on

Friday, 27th Dec., 1929.

at 8.30 o'clock.

Elveden Hall. An answer is requested.

The invitation to the last Servants' Ball on 27th December, 1929.

agreed that there would be a Servants' Ball at Christmastide, 1929, but said it would be the final one. All the employees entitled to attend were pleased to receive an invitation.

There was a large house party for the staff to deal with, but as soon as they were free to do so they hastened to clear the tables and chairs in the dining room and positioned them around the edges of the room, then they had to polish the floor, on their hands and knees, ready for dancing. Then they could go and get themselves ready.

The arrangements were in the hands of Captain Waller, who had Mrs. Waller with him at the Hall during the festive season. In due time the guests assembled with their partners in the long corridor, and at an agreed time the butler opened the dining room doors.

Everyone processed through and were soon seated around the dance floor on delicate gilt chairs. Lord and Lady Iveagh and their family were seated at the far end of the room.

The band tuned their instruments, and then Captain Waller gave the order 'Strike up the Band!' The ballroom became an animated scene as the couples danced around the room in their smart clothes.

When Captain Waller told us it was time for us to adjourn to the Servants' Hall I asked Margery Flack, with whom I had been dancing, to sit with me at the supper. Grace was said, and everyone began eating and drinking. Supper was followed by a number of speeches, then dancing resumed and continued until midnight.

I danced the last waltz with Marge Flack, and she sang loudly in my ear, 'Goodnight sweetheart, all my dreams are for you, goodnight, sweetheart, angels watching o'er you. Goodnight sweetheart, goodnight.'

I escorted her down the long corridor and handed her safely over to her parents to take her home. She was still singing as she struggled into her hat and coat.

It was some time after that last Servants' Ball that my sister Dorothy rang me and said, 'Please can you come down to the Hall now, Lord Elveden's dog is under his bed and is snapping at anyone who tries to move it?'

Doll told me where to meet her in the Hall and guided me to Lord Elveden's bedroom. I put on a pair of gloves and peered under the bed, where I could see a pair of bright eyes watching me. I darted one hand on to the dog's collar, hauled it out and handed it to my sister, who was used to looking after it. She was extremely relieved, as the dog had been there for some time.

That was not the only problem we had with dogs about that time. In December we had some very cold, wet weather, and Mr. Dow rang Dad to tell him that young Lady Honor had lost her pet English sheepdog, and to ask the gamekeepers to keep a sharp lookout for it.

Not long afterwards I saw the dog running into the game larder yard. I caught it and put it in a loose box in the stable, then returned to the house and rang Mr. Dow to inform him that I had caught the dog.

In a few minutes Lord Iveagh's chauffeur, Mr. Potter, drove round with Lady Honor, who jumped out and ran to the back door. I hurried out to say that I had put the dog in the stable. 'The dog should have been kept in the house!' Lady Honor said. I pointed to the door of the loose box and Lady Honor, running ahead of me, threw open the door and gathered up the dripping wet and muddy sheepdog in her arms. The chauffeur held open the car door and Lady Honor entered, placing the dog on the seat beside her, at the same time exclaiming, 'Oh you poor darling, fancy putting you into a stable!'

I sometimes had to ask the butler, Mr. Frederick Cole, the names of the guests at the Hall in order to write up the Shooting Cards, itemising the game that had been shot that day. Captain Waller, unlike his predecessor, Mr. Bland, did not send us a written list. On the day before one shoot I asked Mr. Cole for the names; he told me five names and I knew there should be six. After further thought he said, suddenly, 'Ah! I know, it's the b★★★★ old Speaker!' That was Captain Edward Fitzroy, Speaker of the House of Commons.

Sadly, Mr. Cole collapsed and died whilst playing golf on the private golf course in Elveden Park on Sunday afternoon, 9th January, 1938. His partner was a Mrs. Easter and their opponents were Mr. Robert Ransome, the Hall carpenter, and Mr. Jack Rutterford, the aviary keeper. Mrs. Cole, who lived in London, was contacted by the Metropolitan Police to be told of the sad news. Mrs. Cole arrived in Elveden on Monday morning and the funeral was held at Elveden Church on the Thursday.

Nearly two years later Mr. Robert Ransome collapsed and died suddenly whilst attending a church service on Sunday, 26th November, 1939. Mrs. Ransome later moved from Grey Cottage to 6 Cottage Homes, where eight years later, in the very severe winter of 1947, she collapsed and died after opening the door to Mr. Charlie Paul, who was on his milk round.

The Rev. Graham Napier became Rector in 1938, and he had not been with us long when one day he cycled to the Game Yard and asked me if I would accompany him to the church vestry. He had noted the unusual size and shape of the table there, and wondered if it could be an altar table. We removed the cloth that was draped on it, and he examined the table closely, quickly coming to the conclusion that it was, in fact, the altar table from the St. Andrew's side of the church. After further consultation with Mr. J.A. Dow, the Agent, and other church officials, the altar was reinstated to its former position, where its stands to this day.

Love and marriage 14

DURING my time living at home with my father and family and working in the game office and larder I often had to post parcels of game at the Elveden Post Office. Many times I used to find Miss Marjorie Alderton ahead of me walking to her job at the Clerk of the Works office, and I could not help thinking what a smart young lady she was.

On other occasions as I passed her home to post my newspaper reports I would hear her playing the piano. Every evening I used to hear her talking to her father, Bill Alderton, when she came with him to the stable at the Game Yard to rack up the horses for the night, after which she would accompany him for a walk in the Park.

After a number of years I wrote to Marjorie suggesting I would like to meet her one evening by the gas lamp-post at the entrance to the Game Yard, so we could go for a walk and chat together. She agreed, and we fixed a date. In good time I stationed myself at the meeting place, and soon I heard her quick footsteps approaching. That evening we walked together in the Park.

That autumn was the wettest I ever remember. One evening I stood awhile at the meeting place, then realized it was not fit for Marjorie to turn out, so I walked to her garden gate just to make sure and stood under the dripping beech trees listening. Soon I heard a low whistle, then another, which I thought must be Marjorie calling to me. I hurried eagerly forward, the next moment I tripped over some exposed lilac roots and flew headlong into the bushes. In the pitch darkness I had great difficulty in extricating myself, and by the time I had got out of those bushes I was soaked to the skin. Foiled again!

To my embarrassment, the next day I learned that it was Mr. Alderton who was whistling the dog after he had let it out into the garden for a few minutes.

The remainder of that memorable September was so wet that we later became very fond of the popular song, 'September in the Rain'.

After a year of happy times together I knew I had to ask her father's permission for Marjorie and I to become engaged. I waited until he was at the stable racking up. With fast-beating heart I walked through the door and said, 'May I ask you something?'

Without stopping his vigorous forking of the straw, he said, 'Yes, what is it?'

I replied, 'I want to ask your permission to become engaged to your daughter Marjorie.' He still continued to fork the straw as he said, 'Yes, I've got nothing against you, Ted.' I thanked him very much, knowing how much his consent to my request had meant to him.

During the time Marjorie and I were walking out I received an invitation from Mr. Rumbold, my cousin, to visit the family in London for a fortnight's holiday. Before I left I asked Marjorie if we could become engaged, she replied, 'I will tell you when you return.' With this thought in my mind I left for London.

Visiting the sights of London in the company of friends, the time passed quickly. One high spot was when Mr. Rumbold bought tickets for us all to see a performance of Noel Coward's Bitter Sweet. I was so impressed with the plot and the subsequent thrilling ending that I have never forgotten it. I drew a comparison with my own dilemma, my mind went back to Marjorie and I wondered what her answer would be. On my return I lost no time in seeing Marjorie and asking her what her answer was. With no hesitation she looked up with her blue eyes and said, 'Yes, gladly!'

In December Marjorie and I went to Bury St. Edmunds to look in the jewellers' shop windows for rings and brooches. First Sneezum's, then Baxter's and finally Thurlow Champness, under the clock in Abbeygate Street.

A biting cold wind was blowing, so we were glad to step inside the warm shop to look at and try on some rings. We both liked narrow wedding rings, so that was soon chosen. Next came the choice of the engagement ring, a gold band with three small diamonds. This done, Marjorie wanted me to have a signet ring, but I had no wish to wear one. However, I spotted a diamante brooch which I liked immensely, and when Marjorie also liked it I had the pleasure of buying it for her.

After this my first consideration was to find somewhere for us to live, so I asked Mr. Dow if there was any accommodation available. The first place he offered us was the rooms in the Water Tower. Although the outlook over the Lily Pond and gardens was pleasant, we realized that there would be the constant noise from the water pump and therefore, after some thought, we declined.

The author and Marjorie on their wedding day.

A few months went by with no further word, and then one day Mr. Dow gave me a key to the room at the Stables which the first Earl had used when waiting for his carriage to be made ready. He told me to wait there after church on Sunday morning until he came there with Lord and Lady Iveagh. He told me Lady Iveagh had said, 'We must get the young couple a house!'

They made a thorough inspection of the premises, and as a result of their evaluation decided that a stairwell should be cut through the ceiling to give access to the rooms above. After a time I heard that work had begun at the new 'flat'. The large wooden staircase was constructed at the Clerk of the Works yard, the carpenter responsible being Mr. Plummer. Several attempts were made to get the staircase in position, but finally this was achieved.

One day, after the stair well had been cut out and before the stairs were fitted, one of the young workmen named Leonard Spruce chased an even younger apprentice, Don Cross, along the corridor. Don had forgotten that the well had been cut, and before he could stop himself he plunged some thirteen feet through the hole to the floor below. Fortunately he escaped serious injury.

Much later, after the Second World War, during which he was a prisoner of war in Germany, Don married and lived with his wife Doris and son Stewart in another part of the Stables.

The flat consisted of five rooms, together with a small room with a *flush* lavatory, a larder, and what was a real touch of luxury for those times, a plumbed-in cast-iron bath in the kitchen! A large electricity generator was housed in the east wing of the Stables and this provided the building with 120 volt D.C. lighting. A large boiler provided hot water that was carried round the building at ceiling level in very thick copper pipes that also helped to warm the rooms, which had once been occupied by the Head Coachman.

Now that we knew we had somewhere to live our wedding day was fixed for Christmas Eve, 1934, this being the only day Marjorie's brother Charles, who was a policeman, and Irene Stenning, his young lady, were able to come. Charlie had kindly agreed to act as my Best Man.

When the big day arrived Charlie called at the Headkeeper's Lodge for me, and I made sure he took charge of the wedding ring. It was a bitterly cold morning as we walked down the Park to the church. When the point came in the service where Marjorie was asked 'Wilt thou take this man to be your lawful wedded husband?' she answered clearly, 'I will.' Then the Rector, the Rev. Charles Lynch, said to me 'Wilt thou take this woman to be your lawful wedded wife?' and I answered in an equally clear voice 'I will.'

As we left the church we were showered with rice thrown by wellwishers and friends; confetti was banned in the churchyard.

We had some forty guests at the reception in the Village Hall, and this was followed by dancing. While everyone was enjoying the dancing I noticed that my father-in-law and his nephew, Alf Clutterham, had disappeared.

Snow had been falling steadily throughout the evening and it was bitterly cold outside as Alf Clutterham took us in his car to our new home at The Stables. The house was pleasantly warm and we prepared for bed, only to discover the reason why my father-in-law and Alf had disappeared from the reception. They had prepared an apple-pie bed which took us a long time to unravel; then I found a chamber pot between the pillows!

Of the many wedding gifts we received, one of the most original and delightful was a small terrier called Tino, given to us by Miss Antonietta Diamante. We had great pleasure in taking him with us on our evening walks.

In 1935 we spent a belated honeymoon in Bournemouth, and three years later we returned. We arrived on Saturday for a week's holiday, and during a walk along the clifftop that first evening we noticed that a steep set of concrete steps leading down to the beach was under construction.

Marjorie, always impetuous, decided to go down them, and before I could prevent her she slipped on the top step and tumbled down the first flight to a landing, where she hit her head and lost consciousness. She slowly came round, and I called to two people walking on the beach to go for help to a St. John Ambulance Brigade post nearby.

The St. John officials stretchered Marjorie up the steps and into their vehicle and took us back to our hotel, where I summoned a doctor. After examining her he said that she was badly concussed, but that with rest she would make a complete recovery. The remainder of the holiday was spent quietly!

Our son Neville was born in April, 1939. My marriage to dear Marjorie was to last over sixty years, and we celebrated our Diamond Wedding on 24th December, 1994, when we were delighted to receive a message from The Queen, congratulating us and wishing us a Happy Christmas!

My dear wife died the following June, two months after her 94th birthday.

Members of the Home Guard, including some of the Elveden Platoon, gathered at Brandon. The author and his brother Russell are in the back row but one; Charlie Paul is at the left of the second row, and Harold Wood is fourth from right in the front row.

War comes to Elveden 15

THE outbreak of the Second World War on 3rd September, 1939, soon had its repercussions on the Elveden Estate, in a number of ways. Early in the war the Hall was taken over by the British Army for a Brigade H.Q., and before long there were signs of military activity all around us.

On one occasion a German aircraft attempted to bomb an ammunition column travelling along the A11. It missed its target, and the bombs fell in front of the cottages at Chalk Hall Farm.

I met the Rector, the Rev. Graham Napier, rushing to the scene on his bike. 'I feel responsible for the people's welfare,' he said to me as he rode past, 'they are probably very shaken, and it's so dangerous with all that broken glass around!'

When he could the Rector was quick to secure some War Savings Stamps of various values and to organize sellers for different areas in the parish. My patch was The Stables and the Gardens Cottage; later on I also undertook to cover the Cottage Homes. Number 2 was occupied by two Land Army girls, Iris and Elsa, now of Felixstowe and Southwold respectively, who became very good customers. Mrs. Blower, who lived in the centre cottage, had two sons, Harold and Reg, and always bought a stamp for each of them.

Later in the war we heard that Cyril Barton, who was born and baptized in Elveden, although he was still a baby when his family moved to Surrey, had been posthumously awarded the Victoria Cross. Pilot of a Halifax bomber hit by fighters when on a raid over Germany, he pressed his attack home in spite of the damage and brought the aircraft home though three of the crew had bailed out through a misunderstanding when the intercom was put out of action. Sadly, he was killed when the aircraft crashed in Yorkshire after running out of fuel. When Mr. Napier heard of this award he wanted fervently to hold a commemoration service in the church in which Cyril had been baptized.

When the Rector brought me a booklet describing the life of this brave man, I told him that I knew Cyril's parents, who had lived at Grey Cottage in Elveden Park, where Cyril had been born. Mrs. Barton attended the service with members of her family and many parishioners. Later a bronze jug inscribed with the name of Cyril Barton V.C. was purchased and used to hold the water for baptisms. Unfortunately a disgraceful person or persons stole the jug from the church.

As news of the Allied reverses on the various fronts reached us we began to realise that this war would soon involve us all. There was a distinct chance that before too long we would be called upon to defend our homes.

In the Spring of 1940 the Government called for men not already committed to war service to join the Local Defence Volunteers, a last-ditch force charged with combating an invasion that seemed imminent. I realized that paratroops could easily land in the surrounding parkland, and I told Marjorie, 'I must join so I have a rifle in my hands to defend this place.'

We had no uniforms to begin with, but in due time armbands were issued with the letters LDV on them indicating what we were. Brandon Town became the Control Centre and Harry Skipper, a First World War veteran and ex-sergeant, was appointed to take charge of the Elveden Volunteers, or the Elveden Platoon of the Home Guard as it was soon to be renamed.

The Elveden water tower was used as our first H.Q. On Sunday mornings we would assemble on the grass near the Lily Pond adjacent to the water tower to be taught the rudiments of drill, marching, falling-in, standing easy, and so on.

Other First World War sergeants also joined, such as Ernest Turner, Frank Sharp and Wilfred Bowers, and some ex-corporals. Other volunteers were Horace Crane, R. Hugh Christopher, Tom Trayes, Jack Turner, John Crosby, Fred Flack, Bert Aldridge, Les Lock, Bob Ansell, Vic Harrison, Arthur Wood, Ernie Cousins, Harold Wood,

The water tower at Elveden which served as the Home Guard headquarters until 1942. When the Hall was taken over by the US Forces the Home Guard had to move to a former searchlight site on the Brandon Road.

Clem Gould, John Turner, Noah Crosby, George Crosby, my brothers Ian and Russell, Ernie Green, Charlie Paul, Jim Paul, Ron Trett, Elijah Collins, Les Lock, F. Gow, George Bartle, Palmer Hanslip and Ernie Pye.

On wet mornings we used to assemble in the water tower, mounting the long flight of stairs to the large upper room, which had black-out curtains fitted to prevent any light being seen from the outside. Unfortunately these curtains also excluded the supply of fresh air and the room became very oppressive, so much so that on one occasion young Harold Wood fainted and had to be helped down the stairs into the fresh air.

In that lofty perch, big enough to hold many men, we were given instruction on military matters. We were instructed on dismantling and re-assembling rifles and machine guns, and we took part in target practice using .22 air rifles; why no pellets ever ricocheted and hit us I do not know. The platoon of thirty-odd men was armed with two Lee Enfield rifles and a First World War Vickers machine gun, which had been adapted for use by the Royal Air Force.

Soon we were paired to do patrols at night, my partner being Horace Crane; his second name was Edward, and he was always known as Ted, as was I. We undertook these night duties in addition to our normal work during the day, of course, and as the war went on we became very, very tired at times.

One evening we started from the water tower and had reached the Ice Well when, in the bright moonlight, we noticed a shadowy figure under the large trees in front of the Hall. We watched for a few minutes, then Ted, who was carrying one of the only two rifles we possessed at that time, decided to challenge.

'Who goes there?' he roared. No reply. He repeated the challenge and rattled the rifle bolt as he said, 'Advance and be recognised, or I shall fire!'

A man's figure appeared, hands above his head, yelling, 'Don't shoot, don't shoot!' As he got nearer, still covered by the rifle, he said, 'I've got a girl from the Hall behind that tree.' When we recognised him as a well-known village fellow renowned for his prowess with the fair sex we decided he was no threat to National security and told him he had better escort the young lady back to the Hall.

Another night Ted and I climbed the stairs to the top of the water tower in order to look out across the heaths which surround Elveden. Before the war Lord Iveagh had already instructed that wide openings be cut through the tree tops so that he could have an uninterrupted view from the top of the Hall. These openings also worked for us on look-out duty from the very top of the water tower, reached by a climb up a vertical iron ladder, a nerve-racking task for me and one I could not have done at all in daylight, always having suffered from vertigo.

One night we heard the sound of enemy bombers approaching, being attacked by our fighters. Suddenly the night was illuminated by the unmistakable blaze of a burning bomber in the direction of Bury St. Edmunds. We decided we ought to report this to the village constable, so we climbed down to the big room where the telephone had been installed and placed a call to make our report. A sleepy voice answered, 'I've only just got into bed, I'm going to sleep and I advise you to do the same!'

When our next turn of night patrol came round, we set off along the road passing the Game Yard and on to the A11, turned left and headed for the Cross Roads. Earlier in the war a pillbox had been built at this strategic spot.

As we approached the pillbox we heard excited voices, and then to our surprise we saw a light shining through one of the rifle slits. Ted said to me, 'We must stop this nonsense.' Thereupon he pointed his rifle at the pillbox and challenged the occupants. A sudden silence fell. Another challenge. Still silence. We were in full view in the moonlight.

Ted said, 'I'm going to fire!' The thought of a rifle bullet ricocheting around the inside of the pillbox was enough; quickly the offenders came out and dispersed. We had heard enough to know they were only enjoying a game of cards.

We turned down the Bury Road, the moon looking magnificent above the Contract Covert, walked down the hill past the Contract and then turned left at Summerpit Farm to join Tower Lane for our return journey. Before reaching the water tower we branched right to head up to South Lodge. We had just reached the chestnut tree on the corner of the wood called Home Covert when a brilliant white light shot into the sky and we heard machine-gun fire. Startled, we both fell prone at the foot of the tree, and then we realized that a bomber was firing at the searchlight crew up the Brandon Road opposite where the gates of Center Parcs holiday village is now.

Harry Skipper.

The following Sunday Harry Skipper told us to prepare for a session of rifle target practice at the firing range along the Brandon Road, nearly opposite Spink's Lodge. An army lorry picked us up and waited whilst we were taught the rules of target practice. We were allowed only a few shots each, but at least we were able to feel what the kick from an army rifle felt like.

A Brandon officer with a Vickers machine-gun joined us. He was able to hit the target, having apparently handled them in the First World War and being familiar with their operation.

A week later the whole strength of the Elveden Platoon had to take part in a mock attack through the Forestry plantations towards the Brandon sawmills on the Brandon to Thetford road. Again army lorries transported us.

We were put down in small groups at various strategic places, and John Crosby and I made our way cautiously towards the objective. Soon we were completely lost! A few minutes later we were captured by a Brandon patrol, who took us to the sawmills. At lunch-time the exercise ended, and we all enjoyed an excellent meal which reminded me of the sumptuous teas we used to enjoy at Heath House in happier times.

By this time we had all been equipped with full uniforms. My tunic was loose and my trousers seemed quite heavy, but the ankle protectors were very useful. We were all pleased with our headgear, which was worn at a variety of angles! I had passed my machine-gun test and could wear my badge on my right sleeve. The gun had to be kept at my home for safety reasons.

One Saturday morning we had instructions to defend the Bury to Brandon road from an expected attack by armoured cars. Madge furnished me with a good supply of sandwiches as I had told her I had no idea when I should be back. Ernest Turner called, and we both went off with the machine-gun to our rendezvous down the Bury Road opposite West Gouch, on the brow of the hill facing Summerpit Farm. A small hollow was enough to conceal our gun emplacement.

We placed the gun in position; I was to operate it, with Ernest beside me. Time went slowly by, then we heard the noise of an armoured car racing up the hill towards us. As soon as we sighted them Ernest gave the order 'fire!' and I opened up. The chaps in the armoured car returned fire as they swung round on the side of the road to go back to warn the main convoy. As they turned, Tom Trayes and Wilfred Bowers, who were hidden behind a flint wall, dropped two hand grenades into their open-topped vehicle!

The two umpires who were judging the exercise decided that Ernie and I had both been killed, with the remark 'A very gallant action!' I said to Ernie, 'What shall I do now?' He said, 'Go home and stay there, you won't be needed any more this weekend.' I did, and shared my sandwiches with Madge!

One Friday the entire Elveden Platoon were alerted to stand by; was this the invasion we had been preparing for? I had already planned for Madge and my son Neville to sleep on mattresses in the hall at the bottom of the stairs, as the outside wall formed part of the very large pillars of the Stables archway, which I considered to be very strong.

My station was at the entrance to the Stables arch, and my companion was Bert Aldridge, chief estate electrician, who lived on the south side of the building. He was a Londoner who had served in the Royal Engineers in the First World War. Our specific duty was to guard the electricity power station, situated in the east wing of the Stables. Bert was a chain smoker, and also never stopped talking. While we stood there he told me how the Engineers had placed mines under the 'jerries' and blown them sky high!

After lunch a ground floor window was thrown open and Miss Ivy Ashen, who lived in the flat, enquired, 'Do you think the invasion is near?' We said we had no idea.

Early that evening we heard the air-raid siren and donned our steel helmets. I stayed just under the archway, while Bert was outside, waiting anxiously for something to happen. After a while we heard the unmistakable 'goering, goering, goering' sound of a German aircraft, then the shrill sound of a bomb descending, followed by the explosion. I threw myself to the ground and realized that I was trying to press myself into the unyielding cobble-stones of the archway.

I felt certain the bomb had landed in the corner of the yard. I waited a few minutes and then got up to go and see how Madge and Neville were. When talking over the event Madge and I reckoned the bomb must have landed in the Lime Kiln Wood some two hundred yards away. Next day we were told a number of bombs had been dropped and had exploded in the field opposite the school, on the other side of the Bury road from Lime Kiln Wood.

Harry Skipper called round to see how we had fared. That same afternoon he returned to say that we could relax as the crisis had passed. At this point we all heard a rifle shot. Harry said, 'That must be Les Lock!' and set off on his bike down to Barnham Lodge to find out what had happened. When he returned he was laughing, and told us, 'Les couldn't get the cartridge out of his rifle, so he pulled the trigger!'

Another Saturday at about 5 p.m. I was at the game larder finishing my day's work before going home to tea when I received instructions to put on my uniform and go to the Reading Room as soon as possible. We had been informed of a possible paratroop invasion, and we were supposed to look out for them. I hurried home, donned my uniform and quickly slipped a few biscuits into my pockets. Madge said, 'If you're likely to be out late, I'll take Neville and stay the night with my parents.'

The assembled party was led by Harry Skipper over the A11 and up the side of the 'Jungle', a stretch of woodland at the side of the track. Turning right and continuing alongside the Stonepit Wood towards

Redneck Farm, we were able to see to our left a wide expanse of land perfect for parachute landings.

On the horizon we could see the tall Bird's Hurst Clump, used by shepherds to shelter their flocks in rough, stormy weather. Having passed Redneck we continued, with more trees on our right, then veered right to climb a barbed-wire fence which enclosed a cattle field. To add to our discomfort we found this also had a live electric current to deter the cattle from getting out.

We continued until we came to the 'Carrot Gate' beside the A11. At that point Harry told us we were dismissed and could return home.

By this time I was completely exhausted, the moon was bright and there was a sharp frost and I had already done a hard day's work before I had been called out. Wearily I climbed the gate, then stood with outstretched arms along the top, unable to move. Ted Crane said 'You can't stay here asleep, you'll freeze to death.' Still I did not rouse, so he shook me and said 'We must go home.'

At last we moved off in the bright moonlight. I then remembered that Madge had planned to take Neville to stay the night with her parents, so I said goodnight to Ted and turned into the front gate at No.46 London Road. I tapped loudly on the window near the back door. No response. I tried several more times to rouse someone without success.

It was then that I realized I had left the key to our own door at home, and I would not be able to get in. I struggled over to the Stables and climbed up the stairs to Ted Crane's flat, and with some difficulty roused him. His flat was not very warm but he gave me something to drink. I asked him if he could spare me something to eat, but at that late hour he did not like to wake up his housekeeper, Mrs. Atkins, who lived next door. I fumbled in my tunic pocket and found one remaining biscuit, which I shared with him. After a rest, I struggled back to No. 46 and this time managed to rouse the household and soon enjoyed a hot cup of tea.

Later in the day I awoke with a bad headache and sickness, but I was thankful to have survived that dreadful night.

The real Dad's Army 16

HAVING begun our voluntary service with two rifles, a machine-gun and no uniforms, the Elveden Platoon of the Home Guard gradually became not only better equipped but better trained. In the beginning we did little but drill and learn to shoot, but as time went on the scope of our activities widened a good deal.

One bitterly cold Sunday morning Harry Skipper told us we had all to be instructed in the method of placing the detonators in hand grenades. We marched up the Bury Road until we were half way up the hill past Summerpit Meadow, and there we turned left across the field to a large pit. We lined up and were issued with one grenade each.

A box of detonators was produced. Each man had to take one and, while the sergeant held the grenade, insert it into the small aperture in the top of the grenade to make it live. I was next to Arthur Wood, and with mounting tension I watched as with trembling, icy fingers he finally succeeded in placing the detonator in the right spot.

Harry Skipper and Ernie Turner gave us a demonstration, and then it was our turn. We had to grip the safety lever, remove the safety pin and throw the grenade as far as we could from the top of the pit. In my case, when my hand went back it touched something behind me, lowering my throwing angle so that the grenade barely cleared the rim of the pit and failed to explode. Harry had a spell of firing at the grenade to try to explode it, but the target was so small that it took several shots before we heard a loud 'bang' and knew he had succeeded.

About mid-June the authorities decreed that the Home Guard must get some practice at producing cooked meals outdoors so that we could be self-supporting if we had to camp out. We assembled at the water tower one Sunday morning to do our practice, and were told that our rations were a few pounds of mutton. Ernie Cousins and Arthur

Wood undertook to do the cooking, which they managed with the aid of the tea copper borrowed from the Cricket Club; we provided our own billycans, knives and forks.

We sat under the tall Scots fir trees outside the tower watching Ernie and Arthur at work, and soon a tempting smell began to waft in the air. When the meal was ready we found out why it smelt so good; our mutton broth contained numerous rabbit bones. It occurred to me then that there were three gamekeepers in our platoon. That meal was a great success!

We never knew what would happen next. One March afternoon Elveden Platoon were ordered to go fully equipped with food and weapons on a secret mission. Coaches were our transport to Brandon, where many more men from the surrounding area were picked up, and then we went on to Mildenhall and down the A11 to Newmarket. This time we did not stop there but carried on down the A11, then presently branched right. After hours of travelling, and in darkness, we found our destination to be Quy in Cambridgeshire, where the W.V.S. served us with hot tea, sweetened with condensed milk, in paper cups to drink with our sandwiches. With my fondness for condensed milk I could not resist the temptation to have a second cup.

At this point we were told by a high-ranking officer that he had received sealed orders which he had been instructed to open and read to us at this time and place. We were told that there was supposed to be an enemy force trying to take Cambridge in a surprise attack, and we were to defend the university town. Thereupon we quickly set off on a ten-mile route march, at the end of which we were instructed to file along a short, thick hedge and to lie down behind it. If we heard any aircraft, we were told, we were not to look up.

We were all wearing our heavy khaki greatcoats; I was very grateful for mine, because although by this time the sun was shining brightly, on the shady side of the hedge where we were concealed the ground was covered in a rime frost. Suddenly we heard the roar of Merlin engines as two Spitfires zoomed just above our hiding place. I wonder what they reported to the authorities in Cambridge?

Gradually we worked our way into the outskirts of Cambridge. We sidled up a succession of unknown streets, and then, just ahead, we heard a series of explosions. This turned out to be four N.C.O.s making a final effort before the exercise ended at noon on Sunday.

We ended up on Midsummer Common, where we were addressed by a senior officer, and were treated to some more paper cups of tea and one slab of cake each. For the return trip we were loaded into Army lorries; I remember feeling so exhausted that I stretched out on the hard bottom of the truck to try to alleviate my throbbing headache. I slept until we arrived in Barton Mills, when I realized we had pulled into the back of the Dog and Partridge Inn.

After some liquid refreshment, we were boarding the lorries when

A painting by Frank E. Beresford of the lowering of the Stars and Stripes outside Elveden Hall, with one of the resident peacocks looking on. Flying overhead are B-17s of the 3rd. Bombardment Division. The artist presented a print of this picture to the author.

someone said 'Where's Fred Flack?' I said 'He started to walk on ahead, and said he'd look out for the lorry.' We watched out for him as well as we could in the gloom, but we were half way to the Icklingham boundary before we saw him. Poor Fred had begun to think we had taken the road which led to Brandon.

The Americans arrived in the autumn of 1942, when the Hall became the headquarters of the 3rd Bombardment Division of the 8th U.S. Army Air Force under the command of Brig.-General Curtis Le May. The 3rd Bombardment Division flew B-17 Fortresses from a dozen airfields in Suffolk.

A great camp was set up in the park. Nissen huts lined the private drive leading to West Lodge, and a small single-storey office was built further along the drive, opposite the circle of stones that now contains a weeping miniature copper beech tree and once contained a gas lamp. One of the Nissen huts, near the game larder entrance from the London Road (A 11), remained for many years after the war and was used as a Working Men's Club and Social Bar, and the single-storey office building, too, remained for many years and became a dwelling.

My wife and I and Neville continued to live in the Stables. The stable beneath us was turned into a post office, and a large hut was built on to the wall at the front of the building to serve as the sorting office.

One of the stables was turned into a 'Gas Defense Center', a bicycle pool and repair shop was constructed under the glass roof in front of and including two of the coach houses opposite, and the remaining coach houses became a repair and maintenance shop for military vehicles. There was a large fenced-in motor pool near the Reading Room, and another Quanset hut between there and the Stables was used as a cinema; one very talented serviceman painted some magnificent cartoons on the walls, including a superb one depicting Tom Sawyer.

The field at the bottom of the hall hill, once used by the village boys as a football field and cricket pitch, contained a large number of huts and air-raid shelters.

Often we would have Americans worshipping with us in the parish church. They were always made welcome by the Rev. Graham Napier, and the American personnel appreciated his kindness so much that when they left they presented him with a handsome Preacher's Prayerbook which they had had inscribed. When he left in 1945 he generously left this book at Elveden, saying to me that he thought it belonged to the church and not to him personally.

I remember seeing an American tank driving through the Stables archway; the noise on the cobblestones was deafening. Incidentally, I had my bike 'borrowed' from this archway more than once, although I succeeded in claiming it back on each occasion. Many is the time I opened my front door to find one of our American friends resting there.

With the arrival of the American 3rd Bombardment Division headquarters the Home Guard Platoon had to quit using the water tower as its base because the Americans placed a guard on the tower, the only source of water to the Hall.

We were fortunate that the searchlight unit on the Brandon Road field, near Prince Frederick's Covert, had moved to another site, leaving the outbuildings empty. After lengthy negotiations we were allowed to take over these huts, which became a good replacement for our old headquarters, with the added benefit of no long stairways to climb.

We used to march up the Brandon Road on Sunday mornings and continued with our training under the Scots fir trees, so much a part of the Elveden landscape. The buildings were soon adapted to our requirements.

About this time Victor Harrison was made Officer-in-Charge of our platoon because Harry Skipper had been given other duties, and so had less time to spend with us. On yet another Sunday morning we marched to the large double pit in the field to the left of Old Eldon Road, behind the cottages on the village green, where a hand grenade expert from the regular Army was to demonstrate how to throw a live grenade.

We descended into the bottom of the larger pit to watch the expert throw the grenade into the small, deep pit next door. After telling us about the correct procedure, he pulled out the pin and held the grenade

The Stables at Elveden as they were during the war; the hut against the stable wall on the right was the mail sorting office used by the Americans.

in his right hand. He seemed to hold on to it for a long time, then hastily hurled it into the bottom of the small pit; we heard an immediate 'BANG!!'

The expert looked rather shaken, and we were certain that he had had a narrow escape. He examined the other grenades he had brought with him; they were of a different colour from usual, which indicated that they had a seven-second fuse, rather than the normal nine-second delay. This, he explained as he recovered from the shock, was to give the enemy less time to pick up a grenade and throw it back. It wasn't only us Home Guards who sometimes made mistakes!

The same night we were called out to patrol until dawn the next day. Les Lock and Ernie Pye were told to patrol from Barnham Lodge to Thetford Gap. When passing the meadow near the Barnham road they spotted a white object in the long grass which looked suspiciously like a discarded parachute. Had a parachutist just landed, or was it a landmine? Approaching cautiously, they found a white cow sound asleep.

Some time after this event, Les Lock told me in confidence that one night he had been sent to do sentry duty at the water tank by the Bury Road. He found a large elder bush nearby which gave him shelter. He was tired out, as we all were at that time, and as morning broke he laid back on the spreading bush in the warmth of the sun, and was soon fast asleep. 'If Harry Skipper had come along then, I could have been shot for being asleep on duty,' commented Les.

So much for some of my Home Guard experiences. To a man we were determined to defend our country against all odds; thank God we were not called upon to do so. We all learned something about munitions, made several mistakes, but thankfully suffered no fatalities. We were all proud to be members of what has come to be known as Dad's Army.

We also have reason to be proud of the young women who during the war became members of the Women's Land Army, taking over the jobs of the young men who had to go to war. They worked hard on the land from dawn to dusk and their work was varied and demanding, but they made the best of it and were a jolly and hard-working group; we were privileged to have several of these wonderful Land Girls working on the Estate.

After the war two Land Girls, Pamela Roper, née Watts, and Irene Wood, née Morrill, remained in Elveden. Pam arrived in Elveden in 1939 and lodged at East Lodge with the parents of her husband-to-be, Mr. and Mrs. Bert Roper. After working for a year, hand milking, in the dairy at Redneck Farm, where Charlie Paul was Head Cowman, she moved to Chalk Hall Farm where she took over the milk round from young Reg Trett, who had been called up. The milk was carried in churns, using Kit the pony and a trap.

Irene came to Elveden in 1943 and lodged in the Land Army Hostel at 121 Chalk Hall with several other Land Girls. Her room-mate was Nancy Shaw, another Geordie.

Irene worked in the dairy at Summerpit Farm, both machine and hand milking, the Head Cowman at that time being Tom Baker. She later worked in the Chalk Hall Farm dairy, and also helped with the milk round.

Pam and Irene are now next-door neighbours at The Stables. Pam married Leonard Roper in 1943 and has a daughter Bridget, who now lives with her husband Howard at The Bungalow in Elveden, and two grandchildren, Peter and Kathy. Irene married Harold Wood in 1947 and continued to work on the farm until her daughter Janet was born in 1948. She also has a son David and another daughter Anne, not to mention six grandchildren and one great-grandchild, Reece.

As the war was nearing its end the Rector's wife, Mrs. Graham Napier died. She was buried in the north-east corner of the church, near the vestry steps, the spot always referred to as the Rector's Corner. Soon afterwards Mr. Napier tendered his resignation and retired to Kessingland, on the Suffolk coast.

V.E. Day remains etched in my memory. There was an almost tangible aura of relief and jubilation amongst us when news came through on the radio that the German forces had surrendered. We had come through a terrifying experience, and although it would not all be over until the Japanese were defeated, the enemy in Europe had been routed.

The Americans threw a party in the quadrangle of the Stables. A dais was constructed in the centre of the yard, above which was rigged a large canopy, I think made from parachutes, suspended on ropes from three of the four faces of the building. Flags and bunting were also strung around.

In the evening, when the festivities began, a jazz band on the dais played dance music and popular songs, and ice-cream and beer was distributed in large quantities. My son, then six, was given his first ever ice-cream; when he found out how to eat it, it soon disappeared, and another quickly followed.

Many coloured flares were fired skyward, to drift down on small parachutes, eerily illuminating the proceedings in a multi-coloured light. The children rushed around collecting the spent cases of the flares as they fell to earth. It was a happy day.

The singing, dancing and spirit of goodwill continued well into the small hours, so those of us who lived in the Stables had very little sleep that night!

Mr. J.A. Dow, the Agent, and Mr. H.E. (Ted) Crane, his assistant, in 1951. Ted Crane was often the author's companion on Home Guard duties during the war.

My time in office 17

IN 1946 Mr. Dow told me that he wanted me to work full time at the Estate Office as cashier under the new accountant, Mr. Ben Evans. I was already spending two or three days a week at the office whilst still carrying out my game office work, in order to help my father to do all the necessary paperwork, which he found too difficult to cope with. Later my brother Russell took over in the game office.

For the next twenty-one years Mr. Evans and I worked closely together until my retirement in 1967. During that time I had the pleasure of working alongside some very good people who were all extremely kind to me and always willing to assist me if I needed help. Among them was Mr. Ted Crane, Clerk of the Works and my Home Guard companion during the war.

The war was not far behind us, almost everything was still rationed, and it seemed we had a long way to go to get over the difficulties that had beset us in those wartime years. I had plenty to keep me occupied, for besides my work in the Estate Office my duties as churchwarden took up a fair portion of my spare time.

One of the big events of 1947 was the unveiling and dedication on 8th January in Elveden Church of a memorial window to men of the 3rd Bombardment Division of the 8th U.S. Army Air Force, whose headquarters had been in the Hall.

The dedication service was conducted by the Rector of Elveden, the Rev. Colin Cameron, and the window was unveiled by Major-General Clayton Bissell, Military and Air Attache at the American Embassy. Designed by Commander Hugh Easton, the window shows an airman kneeling at the feet of a seraphim; the background is a typical Suffolk airfield, with Flying Fortresses on their dispersals.

Another window, also designed by Commander Easton, was placed in the church a year or two later in memory of Arthur, Viscount

Elveden, son of the second Earl and Countess of Iveagh, who was killed on active service during the Second World War, together with his batman. This beautiful window was dedicated in 1950 and shows St. George slaying the dragon.

There are two war memorials at the west end of the new nave. One commemorates the twenty-nine Elveden folk who died in the First World War, and also the ninety-five who took part and returned, and the other above the west door commemorates the three Elveden men, including Viscount Elveden, who died in the Second World War.

There is a war memorial for the three parishes of the Estate beside the A11 towards Newmarket, at the spot where the parish boundaries of Elveden, Eriswell and Icklingham meet. It takes the form of a stone column, one hundred and thirteen feet high and crowned with an urn, and the names of the fallen are inscribed on the side of the monument which faces their particular parish. It was designed by Clyde Young and was erected in 1921 by the first Earl, who asked that every household in the three parishes should contribute no more than one shilling towards the cost of its erection, so that everybody could feel that they had contributed.

What a winter that was, that winter of 1946-47. At Christmas we were in the grip of a severe freeze-up, and heavy snow prevented most worshippers from attending the services in the parish church. During this time the Rector held short services in the vestry, the only form of heating being a small oil stove, which together with our overcoats prevented us from freezing. He said that was how it must have been for the early Christians, worshipping secretly in the catacombs of ancient Rome! The icy conditions continued for another four months.

Mr. Cameron, a wartime chaplain to the forces, had arrived in Elveden in 1945 to take the place of the Rev. Graham Napier. His daughter Jill was an excellent cricketer and joined the Elveden Cricket Club; she was a good fast bowler and proved a great asset to the side.

Mr. Cameron told us that he was anxious to organise a Plough Sunday service. With the co-operation of Mr. Dow and the farm workers a very clean plough was placed in the aisle for Rogation Sunday morning, with one or two ploughmen in attendance. During the service the Rector led the full congregation from the church out of the west door, on to the pavement beside the A11, back through the gate into the Park and then towards the memorial tower, stopping at intervals to recite a litany about the beasts of the fields and the grass which the Almighty had provided.

As part of a pre-arranged plan, I was standing at the bell tower entrance when I spotted Lord and Lady Iveagh emerging from Tower Lane, some hundred yards away. I gave a signal to the Rector, who turned towards them and addressed his remarks to them as owners of the beasts of the fields. He then led the choir and congregation along the cloisters and back to the church, where Lord and Lady Iveagh joined us for the remainder of the service.

One of Mr. Cameron's favourite recessional prayers was Drake's Prayer:

> Oh Lord God, when thou givest to thy servants
> to endeavour any great matter,
> Grant us to know that it is not the beginning
> But the continuing of the same until it be thoroughly
> finished
> Which yieldeth the true Glory.

It was Mr. Cameron who was responsible for the inscription around the top edge of the oak table placed in the Children's Corner in the church in thanksgiving for the safe return of so many Elveden men from the Second World War. The words were carved around the edge in order that the children could read them when they sat around the table on the small chairs. It reads as follows: 'A thousand shall fall beside thee, and ten thousand shall fall at thy Right Hand, but it shall not come nigh thee'.

In September, 1949, when Neville was ten, he left the village school and went to Culford School, about six miles down the Bury road. Soon after this Dr. Tom Oliver, of Thetford, recommended that he should have his tonsils removed. The operation duly took place, but it turned out to be not as straightforward as anticipated and Neville had to spend two weeks in hospital, and we were told that he should have three weeks convalescence before returning to school.

Mr. Ben Evans had taken a lease on The Studio in Park Lane, Southwold, and offered it to me for a week so that Marjorie and I could take Neville to the seaside to help him recover. In those days we did not own a car, so Mr. Evans offered to take us there at the weekend in his 1936 Morris Eight saloon.

Loaded to the gunwales, we set off by way of Thetford, Diss and Scole. From there on we were on unfamiliar territory and began to note landmarks for future use, very necessary since there were so few signposts; they had been removed during the war and were not yet replaced. On through Billingford, noting its windmill, then Brockdish and Needham, to the outskirts of Harleston, where we turned right at what we called wire-netting corner, because of the wire-netting fence erected there. At this point we left the main road for the twisting, narrow road through Withersdale Street.

Just before reaching Metfield, an airfield during the war, we rounded a corner and met a pig running down the hill towards us. This was ever after known to us as Pig Corner.

Onward through Linstead Parva to the narrow winding streets of Halesworth, and so to Holton with its windmill set high above the road, yet another landmark. Finally to Blyford and Henham, and then across the A12, where after about a mile it was possible to see the two water towers on Southwold Common. Passing St. Felix School, we soon crossed the Southwold town bridge over Buss Creek, drove up the main street and turned right at South Green into Park Lane.

Our fifty-mile journey had taken us over two hours through beautiful countryside.

The Studio, as it was then known, had been built in 1894; in the ornate oak timberwork on the front of the building was carved 'Southwold School of Industrial Art'. The interior had a gallery at one end accessed by stairs to the side; there was no ceiling, but along the ridge of the roof were windows which afforded excellent light to the room below. At night one could clearly see the flashes from the lighthouse illuminating the upper part of the room.

Early in the morning we would hear activity from Newson's, the bakers, as they began their day. Mr. and Mrs. Newson had a son whom everyone knew as 'Ginger' because of his ginger hair and beard. 'Ginger' was quite a character; as well as delivering bread he would walk peoples' dogs, and acted as a bookie's runner.

It was the beginning of a love affair with the delightful little town of Southwold. During that memorable first week we discovered the Sole Bay Inn, later to become a favourite watering-hole of my father-in-law, Bill Alderton, and Baggots the Butchers. A call at Baggots would be his first priority each holiday, to buy a large joint for Sunday dinner and to put the world to rights with the proprietor.

Looking across the rooftops of Southwold from the gallery of the lighthouse. Just across the road from the brewery in the foreground is the Sole Bay Inn, which became a favourite watering-place of Bill Alderton, the author's father-in-law.

The author's favourite view, looking down Skillman's Hill at Southwold towards the harbour.

Across the road from the pier was the Grand Hotel, empty and derelict, soon to be demolished and replaced by houses. Nearby was the putting green and boating lake, where so many happy hours were spent.

A year or so later my son made a friend of Ben, a retired longshore fisherman who was in charge of hiring the boats on the lake. On breezy days Ben would allow Neville to use one of the flat-bottomed wooden canoes which could be equipped with a small lugsail, and with Ben's shouted instructions from the bank Neville learned the rudiments of sailing.

By 1952 I had managed to afford a secondhand 1938 Standard Flying Ten, found for us in London by my brother-in-law Bill, in which both my wife and I learned to drive.

Our experiences of our trips to Southwold over the years would fill a small book. During one journey we met a traction engine pulling three large fairground wagons, and the road was so narrow that we had to take to the verge to allow it to pass. On another occasion

Marjorie was driving, and the car being overloaded as usual she failed to negotiate one of the very sharp left hand bends and landed up in a hedge. No damage was done, so she simply reversed out and we continued on our way.

On one trip with my father-in-law aboard we came across some very large animal droppings on the road. 'Elephants!' said Bill, and we all laughed. However, about a mile further on, sure enough, we came on three elephants being led along the road towards Halesworth! We all roared with laughter — 'I told you so!' said Bill in between his bouts of laughter.

On numerous occasions we attended services in the beautiful church of St. Edmund's, and were fascinated by Southwold Jack, the strike-the-clock figure there.

Our last family link with The Studio was in 1961, when my son and his bride Gillian spent their honeymoon there, but this did not conclude our happy association with the town. Further holidays were taken at the Craighurst Hotel and other boarding houses, and then at a rented cottage in Lorne Road in 1984.

Neville and Gill continue to use the caravan site at Ferry Road whenever they can, so my connection with Southwold continues, a span of some 46 years. My favourite view is from South Green, where I would stand early in the morning facing down Skillman's Hill and watch the sun play across the meadows and illuminate the church tower and gable ends of the cottages across the river at Walberswick.

Many years later my son photographed this view and my wife commissioned Mr. Arthur Bagot, of Oulton Broad, to paint a water colour of this much loved scene. This picture hangs above my fireplace and is a daily source of pleasure to me.

During the past-war years I was unlucky enough to have to spend two periods in hospital, but each time I came out better than when I went in, so perhaps I should count myself fortunate rather than otherwise.

When in 1951 the Rev. Colin Cameron left Elveden to take another living Lady Iveagh called a meeting of the Parochial Church Council at the Estate Office. A number of applications had been received for the Elveden living, one of them being from the Rev. Graham Napier, who had been our Rector from 1938 to 1945. Their merits were discussed at length without any obvious possibility of a decision.

Suddenly Lady Iveagh proposed the Rev. Graham Melville Napier, saying, 'Better the devil we know than the devil we don't!' Everyone was in favour!

Mr. Napier returned to Elveden with his second wife and took up the reins once more. At his induction service Mr. Dow, the Rector's Warden, and I, the People's Warden, both carrying our churchwarden's oak staffs surmounted by a small brass cross, headed the procession to various parts of the church. I was limping from a sprained knee, the Rural Dean as also limping, and Mr. Napier was walking with a stick, as were many of the other clergymen. The words from the Bible about 'the halt and the maimed' came to my mind!

In 1953 Queen Elizabeth's Coronation was celebrated in the village. There was a good attendance at the celebration of Holy Communion on Coronation Day, 2nd June, and later in the day the Elveden Band rang a quarter peal of Bob Major on the bells of the Memorial Tower, taking fifty-five minutes.

The weather got worse and worse as the day went on, and by the time the festivities were declared open by the Rector the village hall was preferred to the village green. The programme of outdoor sports had to be postponed until the following Saturday.

Nonetheless, the presentation of Coronation spoons to the schoolchildren by the headmistress, Mrs. George, went ahead, and so did the fancy dress parade and indoor sports. Afterwards about three hundred people enjoyed 'high tea' at the school, and all the children received a commemorative beaker.

Another wonderful event was celebrated in Elveden on 19th September that same year when the Earl and Countess of Iveagh entertained nearly eight hundred estate employees at the Hall to mark their golden wedding. Lord and Lady Iveagh had been married on 8th October, 1903, but the celebration was held early to allow a family gathering before the grandchildren returned to school.

On behalf of the guests, who came from the Estates at Elveden, Pyrford, Gilston and Chadacre, my father, then 85 and the oldest employee at Elveden, presented Lord and Lady Iveagh with a 17th-

Tom Turner, the author's father, making a presentation to Lord and Lady Iveagh to mark their golden wedding. At 85 he was then the oldest employee on the Estate.

century gold snuffbox. I remember Dad being very concerned when he was asked to make the presentation, and I helped him to write his speech. After he had delivered it, so he told me, Lady Iveagh said to him 'Very well done, Turner!'

The bells of Elveden Church pealed joyfully as twilight fell on the Park, and the evening ended with a firework display.

Lord and Lady Iveagh later presented an oak altar rail and four Coronation chairs for the St. Andrew's chapel as a thanksgiving for their golden wedding and in memory of the Coronation.

Five years later when a coming-of-age party was held to mark the 21st birthday of Viscount Elveden Dad again had the honour of making the presentation to him on behalf of the Estate employees of an antique gold box and a book containing the names of all the subscribers.

The Confirmation service on 12th December, 1953, sticks in my mind not just because it was a great occasion for us at Elveden. Altogether fifty-one, including thirteen of our own young people, among whom was my son, were confirmed by the Bishop of Dunwich, who gave an impressive address. There were more than two hundred people in the congregation, which included Lord and Lady Iveagh.

During the latter part of the service a fault in the electricity supply in the area threw the church into virtual darkness. My fellow churchwarden, Mr. Ben Evans, and I quickly found some candles and held them each side of the Bishop so that he could see.

After the service the candidates and their parents and friends went to the village hall to meet the Bishop and to have tea. The power cut threatened the supply of tea, but the tea ladies coped magnificently. It really was a very special occasion.

Mrs. Napier became very active in the affairs of the church, taking on the duties of organist, choirmistress and Sunday School teacher. As time went on she took an increasing part in the services, her intention obviously being to spare her husband any exertion, since he was showing signs of ageing and weakening.

On 1st May, 1955, after a Sung Eucharist Mrs. Napier hurried out and went across the busy A11 to open the Rectory gates for her husband. I counted the collection and Mr. Napier signed the book, then I helped him down the vestry steps and out to the roadside, where we waited for a suitable time to cross. I was supporting the Rector, and we had reached the middle of the road when with a tremendous roar a motor-cyclist came into view travelling at great speed towards Thetford.

I put my arms around Mr. Napier and took enough of his weight to get him to the entrance of the Rectory drive. Mrs. Napier was standing at the entrance and took hold of her husband, saying 'Thank you Mr. Turner, you saved his life!'

The motor-cyclist had done well to avoid us. However, later that day I heard that Mr. Napier had passed away, he was 79. He was buried with his first wife. So ended the life of a much-loved and respected Rector.

The Rev. C.J. Newton Gates, a retired schoolmaster who had trained for the Ministry after what most people would have thought a full career, wrote to apply for the vacant living at Elveden. Mr. Ben Evans and I travelled to the School House at Ixworth to meet Mr. and Mrs. Gates, who made us very welcome. Before we left Mr. Gates insisted that we have a glass of port with them.

On the way home we agreed that Mr. Gates appeared to be the man we were looking for, and in due course he became our Rector.

About this time Lord Iveagh had given instructions for the church to be rewired. Spotlights were installed in strategic positions, and these could be brought up or dimmed as the occasion required.

We found the new Rector would often close Evensong with Robert Louis Stevenson's words:

> O Lord God, when the shadows lengthen and the
> evening comes,
> And our busy world is hushed, and our work done,
> Then Lord, in thy mercy,
> Grant us safe lodging, a Holy rest, and peace at the last.

Mr. Newton Gates continued his ministry in Elveden until 1970, when he and Mrs. Gates retired to live in Felixstowe near their son, who had then recently been ordained. Mr Gates died in 1983, and two years later his son John came to Elveden Church to officiate at a quiet memorial service. A plaque is affixed to the wall in an alcove in the Sanctuary, to the left of the Altar, which reads:

REMEMBER
CHARLES JOHN NEWTON GATES
SCHOOLMASTER, READER, PRIEST.
1898 - 1983.

Village happenings 18

FRED RANNS, a cowman at Elveden and a keen cyclist, was instrumental in forming a cycling club in 1954, and several of the village lads became members. My son Neville was one of those who joined, and I was elected hon. secretary and treasurer. Another member was my nephew Edwin, and among the others were Terry Banham (Thetford), Gerald Barfield (North Stow), Roy Budden, Benny Cawston (senior member), Keith Chinery, Phillip Fielder, Rob Glister, Michael Harrison, Roger Howard, Ken Pallant, David Partridge, Fred Ranns (senior member), Malcolm Place (a non-riding member who helped enormously behind the scenes, acting as timekeeper), Arthur Tremayne (senior member), and Bryan Trett.

Club runs were popular, as well as summer evening time trials. The first of these was a '10', the course being five miles out towards Barton Mills and back on the A11. I was asked to do the timekeeping for these events, and in due time a stopwatch was purchased, which made my job considerably easier.

As the boys became fitter, some '25s' were undertaken, and later a couple of '50s' were tried. An occasional massed start would take place, the route for this being along the A11 towards Barton Mills, turning off left on to the private road to Icklingham, then on to West Stow and home along the Bury St. Edmunds to Elveden road, a round trip of about fifteen miles.

On one of these races Benny Cawston, who was a cowman, crashed on a corner in West Stow. Such was the camaraderie of the club that all the competitors stopped to make sure he was all right before continuing the race. He finished second in that particular event!

Club headquarters was the old tackroom of the Game Yard stable, where weekly club meetings took place. I remember the pot-belly stove, installed by the Americans during the war when they had use of the premises, was a devil to light, and produced more smoke than heat. A portable wind-up gramophone was the source of music and rudimentary benches, knocked up by members from wooden cartridge boxes, formed the seating.

Some of the members, my son included, took part in races organised by other clubs. On one such occasion Neville cycled to Wymondham, some twenty-three miles, in the early morning, rode a thirty-mile time trial, met the other club members who had arrived in time for the finish, and then they all cycled to Norwich for breakfast. After breakfast they continued on to Cromer, followed the coast road round to Hunstanton, then returned to Elveden by way of Sandringham, Kings Lynn and Brandon. They arrived home tired but happy from what had been a good day out.

In the winter a coach trip was organised to the Cycle Show at Earl's Court. After leaving the show some of the members went to a pub, had a few drinks, and brought a supply back to the coach for the homeward journey, which turned out to be a slow one because a thick fog had come down. I remember empty beer bottles rolling about from side to side in the aisle of the bus, accompanied by raucous singing!

At two o'clock in the morning, the coach driver stopped the bus and dropped Benny at what we thought was the entrance to Chalk Hall Farm, where he lived. Later that day we heard that Benny had in fact been dropped off at Hurst Wood, a good way from Chalk Hall. He knocked up Eddie Ranns, Fred's brother, and asked if he could borrow his bike to get home, but Eddie, also a cowman, refused to lend it, saying that he would need it himself to get to work in a few hours' time! Benny made his unsteady way home through the fog on foot.

A social and dance held in the Village Hall each year helped to raise funds for the club. During the evening medals and spoons won during the season were presented.

The Village Hall was part of a wooden barrack hut which the Earl of Iveagh had purchased after the First World War. Two-thirds became Elveden Village Hall, the other third went to Icklingham to become their Village Hall. The carpenters and bricklayers, with help from many others of the village, of whom I was one, erected the hut in their spare time.

When the Cycling Club finally wound up I purchased the stop-watch as a keepsake, and I still have it to this day.

Another organisation with which I became involved was the Elveden Village Produce Association, formed at a meeting in the Village Hall in the mid-1950s. Mr. John Whitwood was elected secretary and treasurer and I was elected chairman.

A flower and vegetable show was arranged for 22nd September that year. On the day of the show Marjorie and I were busy staging our entries early in the morning, and when the show opened in the afternoon we returned to see how our entries had fared. I had received a first for my potatoes, onions and runner beans, and I was delighted to find I had won the Smallholder Blue Ribbon for the best collection of vegetables in the show as well.

As I looked at the collection Lady Elizabeth said to me, 'Fancy, peas in September, Turner!' They were a particularly late variety.

That first show turned out to be a great success, and we held another show the following year. This time I exhibited similar classes of vegetables and Marjorie exhibited items in the flower and cookery classes. There was always a friendly rivalry between Marjorie and myself to see which of us had won the most.

Whilst I was looking at my vegetables Frank Sharp, whom I knew to be a good gardener, asked me several questions about the way to prepare exhibits. He said, 'I shall know how to go about it next year', and, true to his word, he became a very successful exhibitor for many years afterwards.

Mr. and Mrs. Arthur Palmer, who were founder members, and later their daughter, Rosemary Flack, were always great supporters of the VPA; Arthur's mother, Mrs. Palmer, senior, who lived in Barnham, won cups and awards on many occasions. Rosemary was secretary for two years until November, 1973, when Mr. Alan Cousins took over in a temporary capacity; twenty-four years later he is still holding the fort! Arthur and Rosemary are still keen members and successful exhibitors.

It was not only the VPA show that I got myself involved in. The chairman of the Church Fete Committee was looking hard at me across the well-filled committee room as he repeated his question, 'Who will arrange the Flower Show?' As chairman of the Village Produce Association, I undertook this assignment, though not without some misgivings because our secretary had left the parish, and I wondered if the treasurer would co-operate with me. I found that everyone I asked to help had other commitments, so I knew I had to cope as best I could.

The Fete was going to be held in the Park, so I started looking for a suitable site to stage the show. I settled on the magnificent colonnade, always called the Indian Walk, near the Hall; I thought by using the colonnade I could save the cost of hiring a marquee, and also the exhibits would be cooler out of the July sunshine. The spot was somewhat isolated, but the putting area and tea tent were set up close by.

However, two nights before the Fete these were moved to another part of the grounds. My brother Arthur improvised a 'Flower Show' notice, but misunderstood the plan for the entrance and cut it three feet short! Meanwhile other stallholders had, without my knowledge, commandeered five of the show tables I had previously set up, which left me on the night before the show in a state of great unreadiness!

Came the day, it was fine but there was a cold, strong wind. I arrived at the open-fronted colonnade twenty minutes late, to find a punctual supporter had left exhibits with an explanatory note. Flowers and vases were lying flat, battered by the wind, with the water spilling across the tables and floor. A good start!

A magnificent entry of delphiniums had to be lashed in their container to a table leg to prevent them being blown over whilst I proceeded with the task of numbering the exhibits, hampered by the increasing force of the wind. Exhibit number cards and bank notes alike were suddenly airborne, a difficulty which I partially overcame by using beetroots as paperweights.

Slowly the entries came in, including the inevitable floral arrangement which did not conform to the schedule, the tomatoes which had been placed in the bottled fruit and syrup section, and the attractive roses which had arrived half an hour late. Show entries were comparatively few, yet heaps of vegetables and bunches of flowers accumulated around me for the produce stall, which I was also running, with comments like 'No time to put them in the show today!' as the donors dashed back to their own stalls.

Just as things were getting altogether out of hand I became aware of a stranger wearing a clerical collar and followed by a lady, who proved to be his wife, carrying a vase of the finest sweet peas I have ever seen. Gladly I booked the exhibit, but alas, after trying patiently to anchor the vase and arrange the flowers; the pair gave it up and decided to withdraw the entry. 'Please don't take them away!' I implored, but they merely pointed out the futility of the situation.

Then I had an idea. 'Let me keep the flowers in my car, and if the wind drops I'll place them on the table before the judges arrive,' I said. Reluctantly they agreed, and left me to deal with the matter. Events overtook me, and at the very last moment I looked at my watch and dashed to my car for the sweet peas; I only had just enough time to stage them before the judges arrived.

Happily those sweet peas were placed first in their class and awarded the special prize for the best exhibit in the flower classes.

The Fete opened, and the exhibitors and a fair proportion of the visitors came to inspect the show. My brother relieved me for a time, and in my absence promised to sell the special sweet peas to a dear old lady from a neighbouring parish, who told him they had been grown by their new Rector. 'He always has a wonderful lot, both in and out of season, and kindly shows the members of the Mothers' Union round his greenhouse,' she told him.

In due course I rejoined my brother, and the afternoon progressed to the music of the roundabouts, the rattle of shot falling on the colonnade roof from the clay pigeon shoot, and the noisy roar of go-karts.

During the teatime lull a friend, Jim Paul, was talking to Arthur and me when — 'Look come here,' says Jim, 'if it ain't old Charlie!' Charlie Turner it was, right enough, having a look at the old place. Straight away memories surged between them of earlier years at this same spot. That seat in the corner, for instance, where Jim had sat in the darkness with his girlfriend, Eva Baxter, who later became his wife, completely unaware until later that Charlie was seated nearby with his young lady. And the cycle shed at the housemaids' quarters, where Charlie had draped the housekeeper's coat over a broom, to the consternation of Jim, the suitor, on forbidden ground, who bolted at the sight of it in the dim evening light.

'Mustn't let my youngsters hear me talk like this!' said Jim. Charlie agreed, and changed the subject to the taking of a swarm of bees.

'I remember when old Alfred Jackson asked me to help him take a lot from a bough, I held the box until they began to buzz around, then I left the scene in a hurry!

'The following day Alfred say to me, "That was a nice way to leave anyone, half-way through a job!"

'I told him, "I never did like those old things, and I expect they know it and don't like me!"

'Old Alfred said, "Go on, I told you when they are full of honey at swarming time, they'll never sting you." A few days later,' Charlie went on, 'he asked me to leave a box near a swarm at another place, but not to bother to stop and help him. Next morning I scarcely recognised him. He was all swollen about the eyes, neck and hands, so I asked him, "What the devil have you been doing to yourself, Alfred?"

'"It's those bees I tried to take last night," he said, "I never came across such a savage lot before!"

'"But I thought you said they won't sting at swarming time?"

'"Must have been some thunder about or something!" Alfred muttered, and walked off.'

With this last tale the two friends wished each other well and went their separate ways.

After the prizegiving the old lady reappeared to claim her promised purchase of sweet peas, which my brother had already wrapped. The exhibitor, we thought, would be back at his Rectory by this time, probably writing his sermon for the next day. Suddenly, to our dismay, he arrived on the scene to collect his entry. 'I've wrapped them ready for you to take away, Sir,' lied my brother glibly, 'but one of your lady parishioners would very much like to buy them.' 'She can see them on the Altar at Holy Communion tomorrow morning,' said the Rector's wife tartly, and they departed. This message was conveyed to the lady as tactfully as possible, together with another bunch of flowers.

Resignedly, my brother and I bought up the vast quantities of produce remaining to swell the Flower Show profit. Although this profit was comparatively poor, the day will always remain rich in memories for me.

You might say flower shows in general are full of memories for me. Whilst visiting an inter-village flower show at Stowmarket, where my wife and I had entered an exhibit, Marjorie had the misfortune to slip on the damp floor near some glass doors. She crashed into the doors, causing them to burst open and scatter numerous chairs which had been stacked on the other side. The noise was terrific.

I leapt to her assistance, of course, and in so doing tripped over the door sill and fell on top of Marjorie, who was lying there unharmed and convulsed with laughter.

A sharp pain shot through my ankle. We were helped to our feet, and after a while collected our exhibit and began our drive home. As the journey progressed it became agony for me to operate the dip switch and clutch with my left foot, and when we arrived home my son had to help me from the car and carry me indoors, where I almost passed out.

Bathing the ankle with cold water did not help, so most of the next day, Sunday, was spent in bed. I struggled to work on Monday morning, only to be told by Mr. Evans after an hour or so later to return home. Eric Peel gave me a fireman's lift and put me into the front seat of Mr. Evans' car, and Mr. Evans drove me home, where Mr. Peel then carried me to my front door.

They then made an appointment for me to see a doctor, and that evening Mr. Spinks drove me to Thetford Cottage Hospital, where Dr. Tom Oliver sent me for an X-ray. That revealed a hairline fracture, and my leg was encased in plaster from the base of my foot to my thigh, necessitating the removal of my trousers, which I then could not put back on. The nurse wrapped a blanket around me and gave me a crutch.

I went to find Mr. Spinks, who was waiting for me with his two small daughters. When the girls saw me they burst into gales of laughter at the spectacle of me struggling with a crutch and holding up the blanket. One giggled 'Oh! Mr. Turner hasn't got his trousers on!'

The girls have never forgotten this episode!

I remained in plaster for the next five weeks, managing to cope quite well at work with the aid of a crutch and a walking stick. Oh, yes, I did manage to wear trousers!

I retired as press correspondent of the *Thetford and Watton Times* in November, 1964, after forty years of reporting local happenings. My successor was Mr. Len Smith, who also worked in the Estate Office.

It was nothing to do with our work as press correspondents, and I can no longer recall the reason, but every three years Len and I would be invited by the Barnham Women's Institute to go as impartial outsiders to their AGM, to count the votes cast for the election of their new president. After refreshments we would be asked to judge the competition for the evening, usually a piece of knitting or needlework.

Neither of us knowing purl from plain or tapestry from tatting, we nevertheless took it all very seriously. It was surprising how many times the newly-elected president won!

When my retirement day arrived in 1967, Mr. Victor Harrison, who had become Agent on Mr. Dow's retirement, invited my wife and myself and fellow office workers to his home for a celebration. Knowing my predilection for tea, he handed me a 'Teasmaid' as a parting gift, and Marjorie was given a large bouquet.

I endeavoured to say a few words of thanks for all the kindness shown me over the years, but my emotions soon overcame me and I was unable to continue. So ended fifty-two years of service to the Elveden Estate.

During my years of retirement I continued my involvement with the Village Produce Association, and also joined the Bowls Club, enjoying many pleasant evenings with my fellow members, who included my brother Ian and his son Edwin, both of them keen players.

In 1970 Marjorie and I became members of the very successful over 60s club, named The Silver Circle. The club ran for several years and many interesting outings were organised.

At the same time we enjoyed coach tours with the Bury St. Edmunds and District Bellringers in the company of our friends and next door neighbours at that time, Jim and Eva Paul. Jim was the captain of the Elveden Band.

Our trips took us as far afield as Wales, which we visited on three occasions so that the ringers could ring at the many beautiful churches. It was a pleasure to hear the magnificent bells rung with such expertise and joy.

'Just the very thing!' The author is presented with a 'Teasmaid' as a retirement gift by Mr. Victor Harrison, who had become Agent on Mr. Dow's retirement; Marjorie, holding her bouquet, seems to think it rather a joke. Photograph by courtesy of Eastern Daily Press.

The author at the age of 94 contemplates a lifetime on the Elveden Estate.

The scenery was wonderful, but I have always suffered from vertigo and the sheer drops at the edge of the roads on which we were travelling terrified me. On one occasion, much to my trepidation and Marjorie's enjoyment, the party ascended Snowdon, the train taking us within reach of the summit.

It was only a short walk to the top of the mountain, but to me it appeared a most perilous undertaking to tackle that path. Imagine my horror when Marjorie suddenly took off to walk up the path; I had to go with her, knowing her propensity for falling down at the slightest opportunity! We reached the top, and I'm sure the view was magnificent; if one only dared look! Certainly a 'high spot' in my life! I continued my work as sidesman and churchwarden, but times were changing. The Rev. C.J. Newton Gates, who was at Elveden from 1955 to 1970, was the last Rector to have sole charge of the Elveden living; subsequent rectors have also been in charge of the churches at Eriswell and Icklingham. The Rev. Ken Dobson was the last to live in the Rectory at Elveden, moving in with his wife Eileen and his family in 1978.

Mr. Dobson encouraged Roy Tricker, an Ipswich schoolteacher and an ardent church historian, to write a short history and guide of Elveden Church. Roy came to me and we spent many happy hours together amassing the information he needed. Roy also preached here, as did Canon Frank Bosley, a delightful, warm, and sincere man, who had spent his early days in the East End of London.

My time as a member of the Parochial Church Council, sidesman and churchwarden came to an end in 1973, some fifty years after that evening I had attended the Annual Parish Meeting and been appointed a sidesman almost by accident.

Mr. Trevor Ede is now churchwarden, together with Mr. Lindsay Harper, who took over from his mother, Mrs. Betty Harper, when she was forced to resign owing to ill health. Trevor's wife Joyce is the treasurer of the P.C.C. and Lindsay's wife Suzanne is secretary. We are fortunate to have such caring and dedicated people, who are devoted to the welfare of the church.

One of that band of devoted helpers was Mrs. Charlotte Wood, who died recently just before her hundredth birthday. She was church cleaner and caretaker for over 25 years. Her daughter-in-law Irene was one of the Land Girls at Elveden during the war.

Another loyal supporter of the church over many years was Mrs. Agnes Kybird, who helped me to collect waste paper and wool which was sold to augment church funds. My nephew Edwin took over as churchwarden from Mrs. Kybird and served until his death in a car crash in 1984 on his way back from a bowls match at West Row.

I was very pleased to meet our new Rector, the Rev. Stephen Abbott, who lives in Brandon with his wife and two children, when he called on me not long ago. I hope he will be very happy in his new incumbency.

Well, thanks to Nev, Gill and now Bob, my ambition to put my memories into print has at last come to fruition. So many people have helped me in this, none more than Mr. Jim Rudderham. I would also like to thank Lord Iveagh for his support and encouragement.

As I sit in my comfortable armchair my thoughts often wander along the pathways of my long and happy life. I've had my ups and downs — who hasn't? — but on the whole I have been a very fortunate man.

My story is told, and while I was writing it down I felt I was actually living it all over again. Living in Elveden, there is a feeling of belonging, a sense of continuity; our lives have interwoven over the years, and although we are two or three generations on, not a great deal has altered here since I was a young man.

Here I am, living in The Stables, in the flat below Nev and Gill, and my good next-door neighbours are Philip and Margaret Fielder. Philip I have known since he moved to Elveden as a young lad when his father Bill became chef to Lady Elizabeth; his mother still lives here.

Margaret is the daughter of Mr. William Speed, who helped me all those years ago to find my way around the Hall, and his wife Lucy, who was a housemaid there before their marriage and still lives in Elveden.

Other neighbours are Ken and Marion Jaggard. Ken joined the Estate Office staff when he was a lad, and now his retirement is imminent, thirty years after mine. I knew his lovely mother, Mrs. Muriel Jaggard, née Rolph, when we were children. Marion is the organiser of the Meals on Wheels team who bring me my dinner each Thursday; the other members of the team are Anne Sloan, Pam Roper (one of our wartime Land Girls) and Linda Gant.

Marion's neighbour is Anne Pallant, a village girl whose father, Cecil Cooper, was also born here; her mother Nancy, a laundry maid at the Hall before her marriage, became a dedicated member of the British Legion Women's Section and other village organisations, and was held in great affection by the whole community.

Irene Wood, another of the wartime Land Girls, lives just across the way, and next to her are Reg and Ann Flack; Reg's dad Arthur was a member of the Elveden Cricket Club when I was a member, and now both of Reg's and Ann's sons, Alan and Steven, are keen players.

As I said, there is a real sense of continuity in our community, and a real sense of caring as well. There are Karren and Wanda, two of the very caring, knowledgeable and cheerful group of nurses who call on me each week and look after my poor old legs. And dear Sue Nutt, who lives in Barnham and sees to my spiritual needs; she has been calling to administer Holy Communion regularly for several years now, in which I find great solace.

Indeed, I am grateful to all the caring, good and generous people I have met over the years, people who have made my life worthwhile and have left me rich in memories. Now I sit here in my chair and reflect on my good fortune. As I often say to Nev and Gill, in the words of Bruce Bairnsfather's 'Old Bill' of Great War fame, 'it's a bit of alright bein' one of these 'ere dukes!'

The Epilogue

In my lifetime I have observed two visitations of Halley's Comet, seen vast changes in the way of life, seen the transition from horse and cart, and traction engine, to motor cars and aeroplanes, to moon landings and probes into deep space and now to the computer age.

I realize that on 21st October, 1997, my ninety-fifth birthday, I shall have been retired for thirty years, having been privileged to spend my entire life on this splendid Estate.

The End?